PREPARING FOR THE
Maryland HSA
Algebra/Data Analysis

David J. Glatzer

Joyce Glatzer

W9-CNC-577

AMSCO

AMSCO SCHOOL PUBLICATIONS, INC.
315 Hudson Street, New York, N.Y. 10013

David J. Glatzer is Supervisor of Mathematics for the West Orange Public Schools, West Orange, New Jersey. He has served as President of the Association of Mathematics Teachers of New Jersey (AMTNJ), member of the Board of Directors of the National Council of Teachers of Mathematics (NCTM), and Northeast Director of the National Council of Supervisors of Mathematics (NCSM). He is a frequent speaker at professional conferences and has written numerous articles in professional journals including the *Arithmetic Teacher* and the *New Jersey Mathematics Teacher*. He has made contributions to NCTM yearbooks and to the NCTM *Algebra for Everyone* project. In 1993, he was the recipient of the Max Sobel Outstanding Mathematics Educator Award presented by the AMTNJ. In addition, he served as co-chair of the Mathematics Panel for New Jersey Core Course Proficiencies (New Jersey State Department of Education).

Joyce Glatzer is a Mathematics Consultant and former Coordinator of Mathematics (K-9) for the Summit Public Schools, Summit, New Jersey. She has served as President of the Association of Mathematics Teachers of New Jersey (AMTNJ) and is an active member of the NCTM. She was the 1999 recipient of the Max Sobel Outstanding Mathematics Educator Award presented by the AMTNJ. She is a frequent speaker and workshop leader at professional conferences and staff development programs. She has written numerous articles in professional journals including the *New Jersey Mathematics Teacher* and the *Arithmetic Teacher*. In speaking and conducting workshops, her interests include problem solving, questioning techniques, communications, active learning with manipulatives and use of calculators.

Reviewer

Diana G. Kendrick, Ed. D.
Mathematics Supervisor, Grades 6–12
Prince George's County Public Schools

Cover design by Meghan J. Shupe
Composition by Monotype, LLC

Brief portions of this book were adapted from the following Amsco publications:

Amsco's Preparing for the Regents Examination Mathematics A

Amsco's Preparing for the SOL Algebra I Test

Amsco's Preparing for the OGT in Mathematics

Please visit our Web site at: *www.amscopub.com*

When ordering this book, please specify: either **R 70 P** or PREPARING FOR THE MARYLAND HSA ALGEBRA/DATA ANALYSIS.

ISBN 978-1-56765-574-2

CONTENTS

GETTING STARTED

A. ABOUT THIS TEST

1. What is the HSA?

Maryland's High School Assessments, or HSA, are four tests; Algebra/Data Analysis, Biology, English, and Government. The HSA test students' understanding of the *Core Learning Goals* that are in the content taught in the courses they take. Beginning with the class of 2009, students are required to pass the HSA in order to receive the Maryland High School diploma. All the tests contain both multiple-choice and written response questions. The results of these tests will tell parents and teachers how well the students are performing in the subject area by pinpointing strengths and weaknesses.

2. When do you take the HSA?

Students will take each test whenever they complete the course. Although the HSA is a High School Assessment, some students may take the Algebra/Data Analysis exam in seventh grade while others may take it in tenth grade.

Currently the passing score for the Algebra/Data Analysis test is 412. Students who do not pass the exam will receive additional help and will be allowed to retake the test during the next administration. Or the student must earn at least the minimum score on each test and a combined score that is equal to the total of the four HSA passing scores. The HSA are given three times a year: in January, May, and in the summer for the students who need to retake the tests.

3. What topics are included in the HSA Algebra/Data Analysis?

The HSA Algebra/Data Analysis assesses Goal 1: Functions and Algebra, and Goal 3: Data Analysis and Probability of the *Core Learning Goals.*

4. What kinds of math questions appear on the HSA?

There are four kinds of math questions:

1. selected response
2. student produced response
3. brief constructed response
4. extended constructed response

The open-ended items (brief constructed and extended constructed response questions) require you to justify your answers by using mathematics and/or a written explanation. The responses can be scored for different levels of mathematical understanding as well as for partial credit. More about scoring open-ended questions follows in Section C.

5. How many questions are on the HSA?

The actual number of questions on the HSA Algebra/Data Analysis can vary between 38 to 50 questions. The exam is divided into two sessions and students have 55 minutes to complete Session 1 and 60 minutes to complete Session 2. The *Sample HSA Tests* at the back of this book are each 42 questions long. Teachers may reproduce the Answer Document on pages 153–159 for the students when they take the Sample HSA Tests.

6. Do you need to memorize formulas?

No. A *Formulas Reference Sheet* is distributed to each student along with the test. This reference sheet is a general formula sheet used for all the mathematics exams. You will not need to use some of the formulas on the reference sheet for the Algebra/Data Analysis exam. Refer to pages xii and xiii for a sample of a *Reference Sheet* that is similar to the one given on the actual exam.

7. Are calculators allowed on the HSA?

Yes. You are allowed to use a calculator when you take the Algebra/Data Analysis exam. A more detailed discussion of types of calculators allowed follows in Section B.

8. How is the HSA scored?

Both selected response and student produced response items are one point each, no partial credit is given. Brief constructed response items are three points. Extended constructed response items are four points. Refer to page xi for more information on the scoring of brief and extended constructed response items.

9. How can you find out more about the HSA?

For additional information about the HSA, ask your math teacher or guidance counselor.

B. ABOUT USING A CALCULATOR

You will be allowed to use a calculator on the HSA. The following information will help you make the most effective use of the calculator on the test.

1. On which questions should you use the calculator?

The calculator will not be needed for every question on the test. With respect to calculator use, questions will fall into three categories: calculator–active, calculator–neutral, or calculator–irrelevant.

Calculator-active questions contain data that can usefully be explored and manipulated using a calculator. These questions may deal with explorations of patterns, problem solving involving guess and check, problems involving calculations with real data, or problems involving messy computation.

Calculator-neutral questions could be completed using a calculator. They may be more efficiently answered, however, by using mental math skills or simple paper-and-pencil computation. For example, the average of ⁻6, ⁻7, ⁻8, 5, 6, 7, 8, 2, 3, 0 can be more quickly found mentally by recognizing that the set contains three pairs of opposites that add up to zero. By the time you have put all the data into the calculator, you could have solved the problem mentally.

With calculator-irrelevant questions, a calculator is of no help because the solution involves no computation. For example, if you were asked to find the probability of selecting a red marble from a jar containing 2 red and 3 blue marbles, the calculator will not help you answer the question.

Determining which questions to answer with the calculator is an important skill for you to develop. Be sure that you do not waste your time on the test trying to use the calculator when it is not appropriate.

2. What calculator can you use?

It is recommended that a student use a scientific or graphing calculator on the test. Calculators with QWERTY keyboards are not acceptable. Your calculator should have at least the following functions:

a. algebraic logic (follows order of operations)
b. exponent key to do powers and roots of any degree
c. at least one memory
d. a reset button, or some other simple, straightforward way to clear all of the memory and programs

3. What features of the calculator are you likely to need for the test?

In addition to the basic operation keys and number keys, be sure you can use these keys:

CE/C ON/AC	clear
M+ M− MR STO	memory
( )	parentheses
+/− (−)	sign change
%	percent
√	square root
x^2 y^x ^	powers

4. What else should consider when using the calculator on the test?

The most important thing is to be comfortable with the calculator you will be using on the test. Be sure you are familiar with the keypad and the functions available on the calculator.

If you are using a calculator on an open-ended question, remember that it is important to show the work by writing out what you put into the calculator and the answer given.

Think before pushing the buttons. If you try to use the calculator for every question, you will waste too much time.

Be sure to estimate answers and check calculator answers for reasonableness of response.

> **Remember:**
>
> Questions on the test will not be labeled to tell you when to use your calculator. *You* must make the decision.

C. ABOUT OPEN-ENDED QUESTIONS

In addition to selected response and student produced response items, the HSA contains two types of open-ended questions: brief constructed and extended constructed response items that require some writing. This section will deal with the variety of open-ended questions and offer suggestions for writing complete solutions.

1. What is an open-ended question?

An open-ended question is one in which a situation is presented, and you are asked to communicate a response. In most cases, the questions have two or more parts, and require both numerical responses and explanations, or mathematical arguments.

2. What might be asked in open-ended questions?

The following outline covers examples of what might be asked in these questions.

1. A written explanation of why a result is valid or why an approach is incorrect.

Example: The average test score in a class of 20 students was 80. The average test score in a class of 30 students was 70. Mich concluded that the average score for all 50 students was 75. He obtained the 75 by adding 80 and 70, and dividing by 2. Is his approach correct? Explain.

2. A list to meet certain conditions.
You might be asked to list numbers, dimensions, expressions, equations, etc.

Example: By looking, you should be able to tell that the average (mean) for 79, 80, 81 is 80. List three other sets of three scores that would also have an average of 80.

3. A description and/or extension of a pattern.

Example: Suppose this pattern were continued.

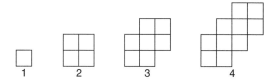

Answer the following.
- Explain how the pattern is produced.
- How many small squares would be in the 100th diagram?

3. How are open-ended questions scored?

On the HSA Algebra/Data Analysis exam, brief constructed response items are each worth three points. Extended constructed response items are each worth four points. (The selected response and student produced response items are each worth one point). Partial credit is possible on the open-ended questions. For brief constructed response and extended constructed response questions, you might receive a score of 3, 2, 1, or 0, or 4, 3, 2, 1, or 0, respectively. In multipart questions, for example, the four points a response could earn are distributed among the parts. The following examples show how the scoring could take place on brief constructed response and extended constructed response questions.

A copy of the generic rubric used as a guide to develop specific scoring guides or rubrics for each of the Brief Constructed Response and Extended Constructed Response items which appear on the HSA is on page xi.

Example 1 (Brief Constructed Response Item): Karin knows that the average test score in her class of 20 students is 80. If each student in the class receives an additional 5 points in extra credit, Karin believes the class average will be 85. Is Karin correct? Explain by using mathematics that your answer to someone who disagrees with you.

Scoring: You would most likely earn three points if you:

a. State that Karin is correct.

b. Support your response with an algebraic or arithmetic proof:

$$\frac{(20 \times 80) + (20 \times 5)}{20} = 85$$

c. Generalize your response in words: The sum will increase 100 points. The number of students remains constant. Hence, the change in the average is the increase divided by the number of students, or $100 \div 20 = 5$.

You would most likely receive two points if you state that Karin is correct and support your response with an arithmetic example, but do not generalize.

You would most likely receive one point if you state that Karin is correct but offer no explanation.

You would most likely receive zero points if you provide an unsatisfactory response that answers the question inappropriately.

Example 2 (Extended Constructed Response Question): A student's score on a math test was determined by multiplying the number of correct answers, c, by 2.5, then subtracting the number of incorrect answers, w. Answer the following.

- Write a formula for a student's score, S.
- Jasmine had 36 correct answers and 4 incorrect answers. What was her score?
- Tony has 32 correct answers and 8 incorrect answers. What was his score?

Scoring: You would most likely earn four points if you:

a. Complete each part of the question correctly.

b. Express the information as an algebraic formula using the variables given:

$$S = 2.5c - w$$

c. Substitute the numbers of correct and incorrect answers into the formula and evaluate:

$$\text{Jasmine's score: } S = 2.5(36) - 4 = 86$$

$$\text{Tony's score: } S = 2.5(3.2) - 8 = 72$$

You would most likely receive three points if you state the formula correctly and find Jasmine's or Tony's score but not both.

You would most likely receive two points if you state the formula incorrectly and find the two scores using the formula you have found.

You would most likely receive one point if you find the two scores but do not find the formula.

You would most likely receive zero points if you provide an unsatisfactory response that answers the question inappropriately.

4. What are some general guidelines for answering open-ended questions?

In answering open-ended questions, you will find the following suggestions helpful:

1. Write complete sentences.
2. Be concise, not wordy.
3. Make sure to explore different cases.
4. Make sure to answer each part of the question.
5. Make sure you answer the question that is being asked.
6. As appropriate, give a clearly worked-out example with some explanation.
7. In problems involving estimation/approximation, make sure you do precomputational rounding.
8. Provide generalizations as requested.
9. Double-check any computation needed within the open-ended response.
10. Be aware that a question may have more than one answer.

Holistic Scoring Guide for Mathematics Open-Ended Items (Generic Rubrics)

Brief Constructed Response Rubric

Score	Description
3	The response demonstrates a comprehensive understanding of the concepts involved. The student employs accurate and appropriate strategies with diagrams, symbolic expressions, and definitions to arrive at the correct answer. Calculations were performed correctly.
2	The response demonstrates a basic understand of concepts involved. The student employs some appropriate strategies with partially accurate diagrams, symbolic expressions, and definitions to arrive at an answer. Most calculations were performed correctly.
1	The response demonstrates insufficient understanding of concepts involved. The student employs inappropriate strategies with partially accurate diagrams, symbolic expressions, and definitions to arrive at an incorrect answer. Most calculations were performed incorrectly.
0	A completely incorrect or irrelevant response. Student may respond by stating "I don't know" or offer no response.

Extended Constructed Response Rubric

Score	Description
4	The response demonstrates a comprehensive understanding of the concepts involved. The student employs accurate and appropriate strategies with diagrams, symbolic expressions, and definitions to arrive at the correct answer. Calculations were performed correctly.
3	The response demonstrates a general understanding of concepts involved. The student employs accurate and appropriate strategies with diagrams, symbolic expressions, and definitions to arrive at an answer. Calculations were performed correctly.
2	The response demonstrates a basic understand of concepts involved. The student employs some appropriate strategies with partially accurate diagrams, symbolic expressions, and definitions to arrive at an answer. Most calculations were performed correctly.
1	The response demonstrates insufficient understanding of concepts involved. The student employs inappropriate strategies with partially accurate diagrams, symbolic expressions, and definitions to arrive at an incorrect answer. Most calculations were performed incorrectly.
0	A completely incorrect or irrelevant response. Student may respond by stating "I don't know" or offer no response.

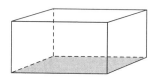

Reference Sheet

Shape	Area (A) and Circumference (C)	Solid Figures	Volume (V) and Surface Area (SA)

Triangle

$A = \dfrac{1}{2}bh$

Rectangular Prism

$V = lwh$

$SA = 2lw + 2hw + 2lh$

Circle

$A = \pi r^2$

$C = 2\pi r \text{ or } C = \pi d$

General Prisms

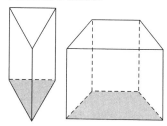

$V = Bh$

$SA = \text{sum of the areas of the faces}$

Rectangle

$A = lw$

Right Circular Cylinder

$V = \pi r^2 h$

$SA = 2\pi r^2 + 2\pi rh$

Trapezoid

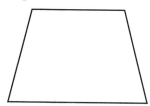

$A = \dfrac{1}{2}(b_1 + b_2)\,h$

Square Pyramid

$V = \dfrac{1}{3}s^2 h$

$SA = s^2 + \dfrac{1}{2}(4s)\ell$

Parallelogram

$A = bh$

Right Circular Cone

$V = \dfrac{1}{3}\pi r^2 h$

$SA = \pi r^2 + \dfrac{1}{2}(2\pi r)\ell$

Sphere

$V = \dfrac{4}{3}\pi r^2$

$SA = 4\pi r^2$

Equations of a Line

Standard Form:

$$Ax + By = C$$

where A and B are not both zero

Slope-Intercept Form:

$$y = mx + b \text{ or } y = b + mx$$

where m = slope and b = y-intercept

Point-Slope Form:

$$y - y_1 = m(x - x_1)$$

where m = slope and (x_1, y_1) = point on line

Coordinate Geometry Formulas

Let (x_1, y_1) and (x_2, y_2) be two points in the plane.

$$\text{slope} = \frac{y_2 - y_1}{x_2 - x_1}, \text{ where } x_2 \neq x_1$$

$$\text{midpoint} = \left(\frac{x_1 + x_2}{2}, \frac{y_1 + y_2}{2} \right)$$

$$\text{distance} = \sqrt{(x_2 - x_1)^2 + (y_2 - y_1)^2}$$

Formulas for Right Triangles

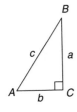

Pythagorean Theorem
$$a^2 + b^2 = c^2$$

$$\sin A = \frac{a}{c}$$

$$\cos A = \frac{b}{c}$$

$$\tan A = \frac{a}{b}$$

Special Right Triangles

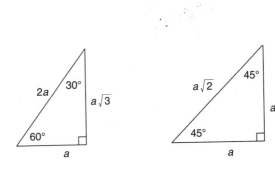

Polygon Angle Formulas

Sum of degree measures of the interior angles of a polygon:

$$180(n - 2)$$

Degree measure of an interior angle of a regular polygon, with n number of sides:

$$\frac{180(n - 2)}{n}$$

Distance Traveled

$$d = rt$$

Simple Interest

$$I = prt$$

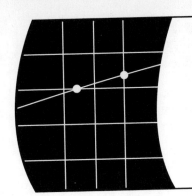

Chapter I:
Number Sense, Concepts, and Applications

1.1 REAL NUMBERS

A *rational number* is any number that can be expressed as a ratio of two integers in the form $\frac{a}{b}$, with $b \neq 0$. This definition includes integers, fractions, and decimals.

In decimal form, a rational number is either a terminating decimal (such as 0.25; 0.165) or a repeating decimal (such as $0.3\overline{3}$; $4.\overline{31}$).

An *irrational number* in decimal form is neither a terminating decimal nor a repeating decimal. Examples of irrational numbers are 0.121221222 . . . ; $\sqrt{2} = 1.41421356. \ldots$ An irrational number cannot be written as a ratio of two integers.

The set of *real numbers* is formed by combining the set of rational numbers with the set of irrational numbers.

MODEL PROBLEM

1. Which of the following is NOT equal to the other three?

   A $\dfrac{2}{10}$ **B** $1.5 \div 7.5$ **C** $1 \div \dfrac{1}{5}$ **D** $\sqrt{\dfrac{1}{25}}$

   Solution: Choice **A**: $\dfrac{2}{10} = \dfrac{1}{5}$

   Choice **B**: $1.5 \div 7.5 = 0.2$ or $\dfrac{1}{5}$

   Choice **C**: $1 \div \dfrac{1}{5} = 1 \times 5 = 5$

   Choice **D**: $\sqrt{\dfrac{1}{25}} = \dfrac{1}{5}$

   Answer: Choice **C** is not equivalent to the others.

2. Place the following rational numbers in order from LEAST to GREATEST:

   $$-\frac{5}{2}, \frac{2}{5}, {}^{-}3.2, 0.35$$

Solution: As you consider placement of rational numbers on a number line, numbers to the left are smaller than numbers to the right.

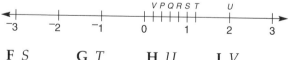

Answer: ${}^{-}3.2, -\dfrac{5}{2}, 0.35, \dfrac{2}{5}$

3. Name an irrational number between 3 and 4.

Solution: There are an infinite number of irrational numbers between 3 and 4. To name one, it is necessary to write a decimal which is non-repeating and also non-terminating. Possible answers include $3.050050005 \ldots$; $\sqrt{13}$; $3.929929992 \ldots$; and π.

PRACTICE

1. Arrange the following numbers in order from LEAST to GREATEST:

   $$\frac{1}{3}, \frac{2}{5}, 0.6, 0.125$$

   A $0.125, 0.6, \dfrac{1}{3}, \dfrac{2}{5}$ **C** $0.125, \dfrac{1}{3}, 0.6, \dfrac{2}{5}$

   B $0.125, \dfrac{1}{3}, \dfrac{2}{5}, 0.6$ **D** $\dfrac{1}{3}, \dfrac{2}{5}, 0.125, 0.6$

2. For a series of eight football plays, a team had the following results:

   +4 yards, +3 yards, +9 yards, ⁻4 yards,
   ⁻5 yards, +10 yards, ⁻5 yards, +8 yards

   What is the average yardage for this series of plays?

   F 20   **G** 6   **H** 2.5   **J** ⁻2.5

3. Select the correct comparison between p and q.

   $$p = \frac{1}{3} \times \frac{1}{5} \times \frac{2}{7} \text{ and } q = \frac{2}{3} \times \frac{1}{5} \times \frac{1}{7}$$

   A $p < q$
   B $p > q$
   C $p = q$
   D The comparison cannot be determined without more information.

4. Which point on the number line could represent the product of the numbers P, Q, and R?

   $$\begin{array}{c}\text{V P Q R S T} \qquad U \\ \end{array}$$
   (number line from ⁻3 to 3)

   F S **G** T **H** U **J** V

5. A fraction is equal to $\frac{1}{2}$. If its numerator is increased by 1 and its denominator is increased by 5, the value of the resulting fraction is $\frac{4}{9}$. Find the original fraction.

   A $\frac{6}{12}$ B $\frac{7}{13}$ C $\frac{9}{18}$ D $\frac{11}{22}$

6. The number 0.67667667 . . . is between which pair of rational numbers?

   F $\frac{1}{2}$ and $\frac{2}{3}$ H $\frac{2}{3}$ and $\frac{3}{4}$

   G $\frac{1}{3}$ and $\frac{4}{7}$ J $\frac{4}{7}$ and $\frac{5}{8}$

7. Which of the following sets contain the numbers 0.33, $-\frac{5}{6}$, and $\sqrt{5}$?

   A Real numbers   C Irrational numbers
   B Rational numbers   D Integers

8. If you know that $\frac{1}{8} = 0.125$, how can you use that fact to find the value of $\frac{7}{8}$?

9. Explain why the decimal 0.33 is not exactly equivalent to the fraction $\frac{1}{3}$.

10. How many ratios of two whole numbers are equivalent to $\frac{7}{10}$ and have a two-digit denominator?

1.2 POWERS, ROOTS, EXPONENTS, AND SCIENTIFIC NOTATION

Exponents

An *exponent* tells how many times a base is used as a factor.

$$3^4 = 3 \cdot 3 \cdot 3 \cdot 3 = 81$$

where the exponent is 4 and the base is 3.

Laws of Exponents ($x \neq 0$):

Multiplication:	$x^a \cdot x^b = x^{a+b}$
Division:	$x^a \div x^b = x^{a-b}$
Powers:	$(x^a)^b = x^{ab}$
Zero Exponent:	$x^0 = 1$
Negative Exponent:	$x^{-a} = \dfrac{1}{x^a}$

MODEL PROBLEM

1. In simplifying $\dfrac{5^5 \times 5^3}{5^6}$, Jessica is tempted to use her calculator to find 5^5, 5^3, and 5^6 individually prior to doing the multiplication and division. Explain how Jessica could use the laws of exponents to arrive at the result in a more efficient manner.

Solution: $5^5 \times 5^3 = 5^{5+3} = 5^8$

$5^8 \div 5^6 = 5^{8-6} = 5^2 = 25$

2. Which of these three expressions

I. 2^{12} II. 4^6 III. $2^3 \cdot 8^3$

is equivalent to the expression 16^3?

A I, II, and III

B only I and II

C only II and III

D only I

Solution: Since 16 is equivalent to 2^4, then 16^3 is equivalent to $(2^4)^3$ or 2^{12}.
Thus, I is an equivalent expression.

Since 16 is equivalent to 4^2, then 16^3 is equivalent to $(4^2)^3$ or 4^6.
Thus, II is an equivalent expression.

$2^3 \cdot 8^3$ is equivalent to $(2 \cdot 8)^3$ or 16^3.
Thus, III is an equivalent expression.

Answer: A

3. Simplify: $(^-4)^{-3}$

Solution: By definition, $(^-4)^{-3} = \dfrac{1}{(^-4)^3} = \dfrac{1}{^-64} = \dfrac{^-1}{64}$.

Roots

A *root* is the inverse of a power.

If $b^2 = a$, then b is a square root of a. $b = \sqrt{a}$

If $b^3 = a$, then b is a cube root of a. $b = \sqrt[3]{a}$

Examples: $5^2 = 25 \rightarrow 5$ is a square root of 25. $5 = \sqrt{25}$

$(^-5)^2 = 25 \rightarrow {}^-5$ is a square root of 25. $^-5 = \sqrt{25}$

$2^3 = 8 \rightarrow 2$ is a cube root of 8. $2 = \sqrt[3]{8}$

$3^5 = 243 \rightarrow 3$ is a fifth root of 243. $3 = \sqrt[5]{243}$

MODEL PROBLEM

$x^4 = 16$, find two values of x so that the statement is true.

Solution: Since $2^4 = 16$ and $(^-2)^4 = 16$, 2 and $^-2$ are two values that satisfy the equation. Therefore, 2 and $^-2$ are each fourth roots of 16.

Scientific Notation

A number in *scientific notation* is expressed as a product of two factors:

(first factor is between 1 and 10) × (second factor is an integral power of 10)

$$4{,}300{,}000 = 4.3 \times 10^6 \qquad 0.000043 = 4.3 \times 10^{-5}$$

MODEL PROBLEM

Compute the product of 845,000 × 0.0000045 by using scientific notation for each factor.

Solution: 845,000 × 0.0000045

$$8.45 \times 10^5 \times 4.5 \times 10^{-6}$$
$$8.45 \times 4.5 \times 10^5 \times 10^{-6}$$
$$8.45 \times 4.5 \times 10^{-1}$$
$$38.025 \times 10^{-1} = 3.8025 \times 10 \times 10^{-1}$$
$$= 3.8025 \times 10^{1 + (-1)} = 3.8025 \times 10^0 = 3.8025 \textbf{ Answer}$$

PRACTICE

1. Choose the correct comparison for the following two quantities: $p = 4^8$ and $q = 2^{15}$

   A $p < q$ **B** $p > q$ **C** $p = q$
   D The comparison cannot be determined without additional information.

2. Choose the correct comparison for the following two quantities: $p = (0.9)^3$ and $q = (0.9)^5$

   F $p < q$ **G** $p > q$ **H** $p = q$
   J The comparison cannot be determined without additional information.

3. Which of the following statements are always TRUE?

   I. $6^a = 2 \times 3^a$ II. $(0.9)^4 > (0.9)^3$

   A I and II   **B** I only   **C** II only
   D Neither statement is always true.

4. If the volume of a cube is 512 cubic inches, which of the following represents the length of an edge of the cube?

   F $512 \div 3$ **H** 512^3
   G $\sqrt{512}$ **J** $\sqrt[3]{512}$

5. Which of the following is NOT correct?

   A $3^8 = (3^4)^2$ **C** $3^4 \times 3^4 = 3^8$
   B $3^4 \times 3^4 = 3^{16}$ **D** $3^{10} \div 3^5 = 3^5$

6. Which of the following relations could you write in the blank to produce a true statement?

   $$2.5 \times 10^{-4} \underline{\quad} 3.4 \times 10^{-3}$$

   F >   **G** <   **H** =
   J The comparison cannot be determined without more information.

7. Which of the following would NOT represent a large number?

   A 5.9×10^{24} C 7.37×10^{22}
   B 3.92×10^{-6} D 2.279×10^{8}

8. Which of the following is NOT equivalent to 5^{-2}?

   F $^-25$ G $\frac{1}{25}$ H 0.04 J $\left(\frac{1}{5}\right)^2$

9. If $3^\square = 9^4$, what exponent goes in the box?

10. What is the missing exponent? $\frac{r^{12}}{r^\square} = r^6$

11. Explain the difference between $a^3 \times a^5$ and $(a^3)^5$.

12. Show how scientific notation can be used to simplify the amount of computation in the following problem:

$$52,000 \times 1,200,000$$

1.3 ABSOLUTE VALUE

The *absolute value* (symbol $|\ |$) of a nonzero number is always positive. The absolute value of zero is zero: $|0| = 0$.

We describe the absolute value of a nonzero number as a distance. Since the point representing $+3$ is a distance of 3 units from zero on a number line and the point representing $^-3$ is also a distance of 3 units from zero, the absolute value of both $+3$ and $^-3$ is 3.

In symbols:

$$|+3| = 3 \qquad |^-3| = 3 \qquad |+3| = |^-3| = 3$$

MODEL PROBLEM

1. Simplify: $|^-7| + |8| - |^-9|$

   Solution: $|^-7| = 7$
   $|8| = 8$
   $|^-9| = 9$
   Therefore, $|^-7| + |8| - |^-9| = 7 + 8 - 9 = 6$

2. Solve for x: $|x| = 5$

   Solution: Since $|x|$ is the distance x is from 0 on the number line, $x = 5$ or $^-5$.

3. Solve for x: $|2x + 1| = 9$

   Solution: If $|a| = 9$, then a must equal 9 or $^-9$. Hence, $|2x + 1| = 9$ means

   $$2x + 1 = 9 \quad \text{or} \quad 2x + 1 = ^-9$$
   $$2x = 8 \qquad\qquad 2x = ^-10$$
   $$x = 4 \qquad\qquad x = ^-5$$

PRACTICE

1. Place the following in order from least to greatest:

$$-\frac{1}{2},\ |^-1|,\ ^-1.4,\ \left|-\frac{3}{8}\right|$$

A $^-1.4,\ -\frac{1}{2},\ \left|-\frac{3}{8}\right|,\ |^-1|$

B $|^-1|,\ \left|-\frac{3}{8}\right|,\ -\frac{1}{2},\ ^-1.4$

C $\left|-\frac{3}{8}\right|,\ -\frac{1}{2},\ ^-1.4,\ |^-1|$

D $^-1.4,\ \left|-\frac{3}{8}\right|,\ -\frac{1}{2},\ |^-1|$

2. If $|x - 4| = 3$, then x equals:

F 7 only   **G** 1 only   **H** 7 or 1   **J** 7 or $^-1$

3. Which of the following would represent all of the real numbers at least 5 units away from 2 on the number line?

A $|x| \ge 5$ **C** $|x + 2| \ge 5$
B $|x - 2| \ge 5$ **D** $|x + 5| \ge 2$

4. Which of the following equations represents the situation: to qualify to be a member of the school's wrestling team, a student's weight (w) must be within 75 pounds of 180 pounds?

F $w - 75 = 180$ **H** $|w - 75| < 180$
G $w - 180 < 75$ **J** $|w - 180| < 75$

5. Simplify: $|12| - |^-12|$

| 1.4 | **PROPERTIES OF ARITHMETIC OPERATIONS AND EQUIVALENCE RELATIONS** |

Basic Properties of Operations		
	$+$	$\times$
Commutative	$a + b = b + a$	$ab = ba$
Associative	$(a + b) + c = a + (b + c)$	$(ab)c = a(bc)$
Identity	$a + 0 = a$	$a \cdot 1 = a$
Inverse	$a + (^-a) = 0$	$a \cdot \dfrac{1}{a} = 1, a \ne 0$
Distributive	$a(b + c) = ab + ac$	

Properties of Equivalence Relations	
Reflexive	$A \circledR A$
Symmetric	If $A \circledR B$, then $B \circledR A$.
Transitive	If $A \circledR B$ and $B \circledR C$, then $A \circledR C$.
Note: $\circledR$ represents any relation.	

MODEL PROBLEM

1. Which property has been applied to allow the product of 15(98) to be computed mentally?

$$15(98) = 15(100 - 2) = 1,500 - 30 = 1,470$$

A Associative multiplication   **C** Associative addition

B Distributive   **D** Inverse for addition

Solution: 98 is rewritten as the equivalent expression $100 - 2$ and then the 15 is distributed over the 100 and the 2. The difference can easily be found. The key is to rewrite the problem using numbers that make mental computation simple.

Answer: D

2. Which property or properties does the given relationship have?

"is congruent to" (for geometric figures)

F Reflexive only   **G** Symmetric only   **H** Transitive only   **J** All of the above

Solution: Since every figure is congruent to itself, the relationship is reflexive. If figure #1 is congruent to figure #2, then figure #2 is congruent to figure #1—so the relationship is symmetric. If figure #1 is congruent to figure #2 and figure #2 is congruent to figure #3, then figure #1 is congruent to figure #3. Therefore, "congruent to" is transitive.

Answer: J

PRACTICE

1. Which of the following does NOT have the transitive property?

   A "is greater than"
   B "has the same slope as"
   C "is perpendicular to"
   D "is less than"

2. Which of the following would NOT be commutative?

   F Addition ($p + q$ and $q + p$)
   G Exponentiation (p^q and q^p)
   H Multiplication (pq and qp)
   J All of the above are commutative.

3. For the following relationship, which properties would be TRUE?

   "is perpendicular to" (for lines)

   A Reflexive only
   B Symmetric only
   C Transitive only
   D Reflexive, symmetric, and transitive

4. For which of the following could the distributive property be used to rewrite the expression?

   F $a + (b - c)$ **H** $a - (b \div c)$
   G $a(b - c)$ **J** $ab - c$

5. Which relation has all three equivalence properties?

   A "has the same grandmother as"
   B "is in the same time zone as"
   C "has at least as many calories as"
   D "lives across the street from"

6. Deanne bought 6 tee shirts at $8.95 each. She figured out her total purchase by using a short-cut: $6 \times \$9 - 6 \times \$0.05 = \$53.70$. Her shortcut is an illustration of which property?

1.5 PRIMES, FACTORS, AND MULTIPLES

Numbers can be classified as *prime* or *composite*.

A *prime number* is a whole number greater than 1 with exactly two factors, 1 and the number.

$$2, 3, 5, 7, 11, 13, \ldots$$

A *composite number* is a whole number greater than 1 with more than two factors.

$$4, 6, 8, 9, 10, 12, \ldots$$

One number is a *factor* of another number if it evenly divides that number.
Thus, 6 is a factor of 18, since $18 \div 6 = 3$.
But 8 is not a factor of 18, since $18 \div 8$ is not equal to a whole number.
Two or more numbers may share common factors.
The largest shared common factor is called the **greatest common factor (GCF)**. The GCF of 18 and 48 is 6.
A *multiple* of a number is the product of that number and any other whole number.
Thus, 20 is a multiple of 5, since $4 \times 5 = 20$.
But 18 is not a multiple of 4, since no whole number times 4 equals 18.
Two or more numbers may share a common multiple.
The smallest shared common multiple is called the **least common multiple (LCM)**. The LCM of 12 and 15 is 60.

MODEL PROBLEM

1. Mr. Smart likes to describe his age in the following way: "If you divide my age by 7, the remainder is 1. If you divide my age by 2, the remainder is 1. If you divide my age by 3, the remainder is 1. My age is not divisible by 5 and is less than 100. Now you know my age." How old is Mr. Smart?

Solution:

If Mr. Smart's age is divisible by 7, 2, and 3, his age would be $7 \cdot 3 \cdot 2 = 42$

To obtain a remainder of 1 on each division, his age must be $42 + 1$ or 43.
No other possible age fits the conditions.

Answer: 43

2. The members of the Decorating Committee for a school dance have 36 red carnations, 48 white carnations, and 60 pink carnations. They want to form identical centerpieces, using all of the carnations, so that each one has the same combination of colors as the other centerpieces. What is the largest number of centerpieces they can make?

Solution: Factor each number.

red: 36: (1, 2, 3, 4, 6, 9, 12, 18, 36)
white: 48: (1, 2, 3, 4, 6, 8, 12, 16, 24, 48)
pink: 60: (1, 2, 3, 4, 5, 6, 10, 12, 15, 20, 30, 60)
common factors: (1, 2, 3, 4, 6, 12)

Answer: GCF = 12

3. What is the least number of pencils that could be packaged evenly in groups of 8 pencils OR groups of 12 pencils?

Solution:

packages of 8 could hold: (8, 16, 24, 32, 40, 48, . . .)
packages of 12 could hold: (12, 24, 36, 48, 60, . . .)

Answer: Least number possible is 24.

PRACTICE

1. Which of the numbers below has all the following characteristics?

- It is a multiple of 12.
- It is the least common multiple of two one-digit even numbers.
- It is not a factor of 36.

A 12   B 24   C 36   D 48

2. Which of the following is NOT a correct statement?

F If *a* is a multiple of *b*, then *b* is a factor of *a*.
G If *b* is a factor of *a*, then *b* is a multiple of *a*.
H Any two numbers can have a common multiple.
J If *a* is a multiple of *b* and *b* is a multiple of *c*, then *a* is a multiple of *c*.

3. 48 is NOT a multiple of 36 because

  A 12 is the greatest common factor of 48 and 36.
  B 9 is a factor of 36 but not a factor of 48.
  C 48 is not a prime number.
  D No whole number multiplied by 36 will give a product of 48.

4. 18 is NOT a factor of 84 because

  F 84 is not prime.
  G 18 is not prime.
  H 6 is not a factor of 84.
  J 9 is not a factor of 84.

5. What is the smallest three-digit number divisible by 3?

6. If 2, 3, and 5 are factors of a number, list three other factors of the number.

7. Lisa believes that a characteristic of a prime number is that prime numbers are odd. Explain why Lisa's generalization is incorrect.

8. If 2 is not a factor of a number, why can't 6 be a factor of the same number?

9. One rectangle has an area of 48 cm². Another rectangle has an area of 80 cm². The dimensions of each rectangle are whole numbers. If each rectangle is to have the same length, what is the greatest possible dimension, in centimeters, the length can be?

10. Jack believes that the larger a number is, the more factors the number has. Write an argument in support or contradiction of Jack's belief.

11. Chen believes that the LCM of two numbers is always greater than either number. Write an argument in support or contradiction of Chen's belief.

12. Stan and John begin a race at the same time. John runs a lap of the track in 8 minutes. Stan runs the same lap in 6 minutes. When is the first time that John and Stan will complete a lap together?

1.6 RATIO AND PROPORTION

A **ratio** is a comparison of two numbers by division.
  The ratio of two numbers a and b (where $b \neq 0$) can be expressed as:

$$a \text{ to } b \quad \text{or} \quad a : b \quad \text{or} \quad \frac{a}{b}$$

A ratio that compares two unlike quantities is called a **rate**.
A **proportion** is a statement that two ratios are equal.
  In a proportion, the **cross products** are equal.

$$Example: \quad \frac{2}{3} = \frac{8}{12}$$
$$2 \times 12 = 3 \times 8$$

To Find a Unit Rate:

1. Set up a ratio comparing the given units.
2. Divide to find the rate for one unit of the given quantity.

MODEL PROBLEM

1. Find the unit rate if you travel 150 miles in 2.5 hours.

Solution: $\dfrac{\text{miles} \rightarrow}{\text{hours} \rightarrow} \dfrac{150}{2.5} = \dfrac{1{,}500}{25} = \dfrac{60}{1}$

Answer: The rate is 60 mph.

2. A store has a 10-oz. package of oat cereal for $2.29 and a 15-oz. package of the same cereal for $2.89. Which is the better buy?

Solution:

$$\dfrac{\text{price} \rightarrow}{\text{oz.} \rightarrow} \dfrac{2.29}{10} = \dfrac{0.229}{1} = 0.229 \text{ cent/oz.}$$

$$\dfrac{\text{price} \rightarrow}{\text{oz.} \rightarrow} \dfrac{2.89}{15} = \dfrac{0.193}{1} = 0.193 \text{ cent/oz.}$$

Answer: The 15-oz. package is the better buy.

3. Solve: $\dfrac{1.2}{1.5} = \dfrac{x}{5}$

Solution: $(1.5)(x) = (1.2)(5)$

$$1.5x = 6$$
$$x = \dfrac{6}{1.5}$$

Answer: $x = 4$

4. In the scale on a map, 1 cm represents 250 km. What is the actual distance represented by a length of 1.75 cm?

Solution: $\dfrac{\text{cm} \rightarrow}{\text{km} \rightarrow} \dfrac{1}{250} = \dfrac{1.75}{x}$

$$x = (1.75)(250)$$

Answer: $x = 437.5$ km

PRACTICE

1. In a class of 25 students, there are 13 boys. What is the ratio of girls to boys?

   A $12:13$ **B** $12:25$ **C** $13:12$ **D** $13:25$

2. John is paid at the rate of $8.50 an hour for the first 40 hours a week that he works. He is paid time and a half for any hours over 40. What would John's gross pay be for a week in which he worked 48 hours?

   F $340 **G** $408 **H** $442 **J** $610

3. A basketball player makes 3 out of every 5 of her foul shots. At this rate, if she attempts 55 foul shots, how many will she miss?

   A 50 **B** 40 **C** 33 **D** 22

4. If three students share $180 in the ratio $1:2:3$, how much is the largest share?

   F $30 **G** $60 **H** $90 **J** $120

5. In a recipe, 4 eggs are used to make 36 muffins. How many eggs are needed to make 90 muffins?

   A 8 **B** 9 **C** 10 **D** 12

6. If 30 cards can be printed in 40 minutes, how many hours will it take to print 540 cards at the same rate?

   F 6 hours **H** 12 hours
   G 9 hours **J** 15 hours

7. Which proportion does NOT represent the given question?

    If 48 oz. cost $1.89, what will 72 oz. cost?

    A $\dfrac{48}{1.89} = \dfrac{72}{x}$ **C** $\dfrac{1.89}{72} = \dfrac{x}{48}$

    B $\dfrac{48}{72} = \dfrac{1.89}{x}$ **D** $\dfrac{1.89}{48} = \dfrac{x}{72}$

8. With which roll of film would the cost of a single exposure be less? By how much less would it be?

    a roll of 20-exposure film for $2.30
    a roll of 12-exposure film for $1.50

    F 20 exposures, $0.08
    G 20 exposures, $0.01
    H 12 exposures, $0.80
    J 12 exposures, $0.01

9. Which of the following is a better buy? Explain why.

    a 3-pack of blank videotapes for $8.85
    a 2-pack of blank videotapes for $5.95

10. Which of the following situations represents a better salary offer? Explain why.

    a salary of $504.50 per week
    $12.50 per hour for 40 hours

11. One car travels 468 miles on 18 gallons of gas. Will 40 gallons of gas be enough for the car to travel 1,200 miles? Explain.

12. Solve the given proportion. $\dfrac{28}{32} = \dfrac{x}{40}$

13. The scale on a map is $\dfrac{1}{2}$ inch = 55 miles. How far apart are two cities that are shown as being 5 inches apart on the map?

1.7   PERCENT

Percent means per hundred $\left(\% \text{ symbol} = \dfrac{1}{100}\right)$. A percent is a ratio that compares a number to 100.

A percent can be written as a fraction or as a decimal.

$$25\% = 0.25 = \dfrac{1}{4}$$

> **Key Percents to Remember:**
> 100% is all.
> 50% is one-half.
> 25% is one-quarter.
> 10% is one-tenth.
> 1% is one-hundredth.
> 200% is double.

MODEL PROBLEM

Barry's restaurant check for dinner totaled $18 before the tip. He wanted to leave a 15% tip. Explain how Barry would be able to compute the tip mentally.

Solution: 15% = 10% + 5%

10% of $18 = $1.80   5% of $18 = $\dfrac{1}{2}$ of 10% of $18 = $0.90

Answer: 15% of $18 = $2.70

In general, percent applications involve three terms:

percentage: part of the total   *rate:* percent   *base:* total amount

To solve percent problems, use the formula: ***percentage = rate × base***

MODEL PROBLEM

1. At a sale, Dan paid $59 for a sweater whose price had been reduced 20%. What was the original price?

Solution:

20% reduction → sale price is 80% of original price

59 is 80% of original price

$$p = r \times b$$
$$59 = 0.80 \times b$$
$$\frac{59}{0.80} = b$$

Answer: $73.75 = b

2. The price of a shirt increased from $20 to $25. Find the percent of increase.

Solution:

$$\text{percent increase} = \frac{\text{increase}}{\text{original amount}},$$
$$\text{expressed as a percent}$$

$$\text{percent increase} = \frac{25 - 20}{20}$$

$$= \frac{5}{20} = \frac{1}{4} = 25\%$$

Answer: $\frac{1}{4}$ expressed as a percent is 25%

PRACTICE

1. The number of students in the senior class is 240. This figure is 112% of what it was the previous year. This means that:

   A 12 more students are in the senior class now.
   B The number of students in the senior class decreased from last year to this year.
   C The total population of the school increased.
   D The number of seniors increased from last year to this year.

2. Which of the following is NOT a correct statement?

   F 63% of 63 is less than 63.
   G 115% of 63 is more than 63.
   H $\frac{1}{3}$% of 63 is the same as $\frac{1}{3}$ of 63.
   J 100% of 63 is equal to 63.

3. On a math test of 25 questions, Mary scored 72%. How many questions did Mary get wrong?

   A 7   B 9   C 18   D 20

4. Laura bought a softball glove at 40% off the original price. This discount saved her $14.40. What was the original price of the glove?

   F $5.76 **G** $20.16 **H** $36 **J** $50.40

5. The sale price of a chair is $510 after a 15% discount has been given. Find the original price.

   A $76.50 **B** $433.50 **C** $586.50 **D** $600

6. The regular price of an exercise bike is $125. If it is on sale for 40% off the regular price, what is the sale price?

   F $90 **G** $80 **H** $75 **J** $48

7. The Sound System Store is selling AM-FM radios for $\frac{1}{3}$ off the regular price of $63. Murphy's Discount Store is selling the same radios at 25% off the regular price of $60. What is the lower sale price for the radio?

   A $35 **B** $42 **C** $45 **D** $48

8. If a price is doubled, it is increased by ___%.

9. If you needed to compute $33\frac{1}{3}$% of $45 without a calculator, would it be better to represent $33\frac{1}{3}$% as a fraction or a decimal? Explain your response.

10. When the sales-tax rate decreased from 7% to 6%, how much less in sales tax did you pay in purchasing an item priced at $480?

11. To obtain a score of 75% on a test containing 40 questions, how many questions must Juan get correct?

12. On a 10 × 10 grid, 31 squares are shaded. How many squares would have to be shaded on a 5 × 10 grid in order to have the same percent of the total squares shaded?

13. The cost of a first-class stamp increased from 37¢ to 39¢. Find the percent of increase.

14. The enrollment in a school went from 750 students to 600 students over a 10-year period. Find the percent of decrease.

15. Using the simple interest formula, $I = PRT$, what is the interest on $400 borrowed at 6% for 2 years?

16. Norma received a commission of 5% on her sales. Her gross sales for November were $12,500. How much more would she receive if her commission were raised to 7%?

17. Is there a difference between buying an item at 50% off the regular price versus buying an item reduced by 30%, and then reduced by an additional 20%? Give examples to justify your answer.

Assessment   Chapter 1

1. Which of the following types of numbers would solve the equation $x^2 = 45$?

   A Whole numbers **C** Integers
   B Rational numbers **D** Irrational numbers

2. Which of the following equations represents the following situation: to qualify to be a member of the school's math team, a student's cumulative points on a qualifying exam must be within 15 points of 275?

   F $|x - 15| \leq 275$ **H** $x - 15 \leq 275$
   G $x - 275 \leq 15$ **J** $|x - 275| \leq 15$

3. Which of the following represents a commutative operation?

   A $a * b = a^2 - b$　　**C** $a * b = a^b$
   B $a * b = 4(a + b)$　　**D** $a * b = a \div (3b)$

4. Which of the following is NOT equal to the other three?

   F 1.5×10^1　**G** $\dfrac{15}{10}$　**H** 150%　**J** $\sqrt{2.25}$

5. Which of the following numbers is between $\dfrac{1}{10,000}$ and $\dfrac{1}{100,000}$, and is also correctly expressed in scientific notation?

   A 4.5×10^{-3}　　**C** 4.5×10^{-4}
   B 4.5×10^{3}　　**D** 4.5×10^{-5}

6. A $32 sweater is reduced by 25% for a holiday sale. By what percent must the sale price of the sweater be multiplied to restore the price to the original price before the sale?

   F $133\frac{1}{3}\%$　**G** 125%　**H** 25%　**J** 8%

7. The members of the Decorating Committee for a school dance have 24 red carnations, 32 white carnations, and 40 pink carnations. They want to form as many identical centerpieces as possible, using all of the carnations so that each centerpiece has the same combination of colors as all of the other centerpieces. How many pink carnations will each centerpiece have?

   A 4　　**B** 5　　**C** 8　　**D** 10

8. Which of the following is NOT a way to find 120% of a number?

   F Multiply the number by 1.20.
   G Divide the number by 5 and add the result to the number.
   H Divide the number by 5 and multiply the result by 6.
   J Multiply the number by 0.20 and multiply the result by 5.

9. On some days, a bakery packages cupcakes 4 to a package. On other days, cupcakes are packaged in packages of 6 or 8. On a given day, all of the cupcakes baked were packaged and there was one cupcake left over. Which of the following could NOT be the number of cupcakes baked on that day?

   A 22　　**B** 25　　**C** 49　　**D** 97

10. There are three times as many girls as boys in the Spanish Club of Central High School. If there are 36 members in the club, how many of them are boys?

    F 9　　**G** 12　　**H** 15　　**J** 27

11. Light travels at a speed of about 186,281.7 miles per second. How far would light travel in 365 days?

    A 5.87×10^{12} miles
    B 6.79×10^{7} miles
    C 7.05×10^{13} miles
    D 9.7×10^{10} miles

12. Mr. Kim, a salesperson, is paid $300 a week plus commission. His commission is 5% of his weekly sales. In the month of January, his weekly sales totals were:

Week 1	Week 2	Week 3	Week 4
$8,576	$9,500	$7,362	$10,567

    What is his average weekly commission?

    F $429　**G** $450　**H** $528　**J** $1,800

13. Knowing that $2^3 = 2 \times 2 \times 2 = 8$, what number in the box would make the following TRUE?

    $$8^6 = 2^{\square}$$

    A 9　　**B** 15　　**C** 18　　**D** 24

14. Miranda earns $7.50 an hour for the first 40 hours a week she works. She earns time and a half for any hours over 40 she works during the week and double time for hours worked on the weekend. Her time card for one week is shown below. How much did Miranda earn?

Mon.	Tues.	Wed.	Thurs.	Fri.	Sat.
$8\frac{1}{2}$	9	$9\frac{1}{2}$	8	7	$3\frac{1}{2}$

F $341.25   H $375

G $361.88   J $382.50

15. A fraction is equivalent to $\frac{3}{8}$. The sum of the numerator and denominator is 33. What is the fraction?

16. Suppose you visited Canada and took $325 to spend. The rate of currency exchange was $1.1515 Canadian dollars per U.S. dollar. To the nearest dollar, how many Canadian dollars would you get for the exchange?

17. Helene is paid at the rate of $6.50 an hour for the first 40 hours a week that she works. She is paid time and a half for any hours over 40. How much more will Helene make working 50 hours compared with working 46 hours?

18. If five students share $450 in the ratio 1 : 2 : 3 : 4 : 5, how much is the largest share?

19. A baseball player's batting average is the ratio of the number of hits to the official number of times at bat. A player had 150 hits during a season and wound up with a batting average of .300. What was the total number of times he was officially at bat for the season?

20. A printer charges 4.2 cents per copy of a standard size original. There is an additional charge of one-half cent for each copy on colored paper. How much would you pay for 100 copies of an original on white paper and 100 copies on blue paper?

21. Ground beef sells for $2.19 per pound. If a package of ground beef costs $4.25, what is the weight of the package to the nearest hundredth of a pound?

22. Because of a printer malfunction, Harold could not read some of the information on the monthly statement from his checking account. From the information given, find the closing balance of Harold's account.

Account Summary		
Number 00-537-387-5		
Beginning balance 08/01		875.45
3 deposits/credits		xxxxxxx
3 checks/debits		xxxxxxx
service charge		xxxxxxx
Ending balance 08/31		

Date	Amount	Date	Amount
08/02	135.00+	08/22	35.92−
08/05	163.50−	08/25	214.35+
08/11	14.75−	08/29 printing checks	11.45−
		08/31 interest	3.45+

23. Mary puts $1,500 in a bank certificate that pays an annual rate of 4.5% compounded annually. No withdrawals or deposits are made. How much will the certificate be worth (to the nearest dollar) at the end of 7 years?

24. If a principal of $1,000 is saved at an annual yield of 8% and the interest is kept in the account, in how many years will the principal double in value?

25. The cost of a hamburger goes from $2.00 to $2.25. Determine the percent of increase. Explain your approach.

26. In York City, the sales-tax rate is increased from 7% to 7.25%. Under this change, how much additional tax would you pay in purchasing an item priced at $800? Show your process in determining the answer.

27. The scale on a map is $\frac{1}{2}$ inch = 80 miles. How far apart are two cities that are $4\frac{3}{4}$ inches apart on the map? Explain your answer and approach.

28. If 4, 5, and 7 are factors of a number, list four other numbers that would also be factors of the number.

29. Your friend applies the Distributive Property to multiplication and determines $2(3 \times 5) = 2(3) \times 2(5)$. Write a paragraph explaining how you would convince your friend that he is incorrect.

30. Every Monday, at Capri Pizza, lucky customers can get free slices of pizza and free soda. Every 10th customer gets a free plain slice of pizza and every 12th customer gets a free cup of soda. On the first Monday of March, Capri Pizza had 211 customers. Answer the following:

    • How many free pizza slices were given away? How many cups of soda were given away?
    • When Jackie came into Capri Pizza, the owner told her that she was the first person to get both free items (the free slice of pizza and the free soda). What number customer must Jackie have been? How many other customers (from the 211 customers) would also get both free items?
    • Suppose the owner also decides to give away free bag of potato chips to every 7th customer. Would any of the 211 customers be lucky enough to get all three free items? Explain.

31. Your local supermarket offers two brands of cheese sticks:

    Brand A: 12-ounce package for $2.49
    Brand B: 15-ounce package for $3.19

    Answer the following:

    • Which is the better buy? Show how you arrived at your answer.
    • Suppose the one that is a better buy now has a 10% price increase. Is it still the better buy? Explain.

32. Given: $0.4 < A < 0.5$

    $0.7 < B < 0.9$

    $0 < C < 0.1$

    $1 < D < 2$

    $4 < E < 5$

    If $X = A + B$, note that the number line shows a possible location of X.

Using the number line below, insert a mark and a capital letter to show one possible location for each of the following:

    • P if $P = A \times B$
    • Q if $Q = B^2$
    • R if $R = 3C - 3D$
    • S if $S = \sqrt{E}$

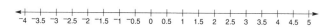

Explain your locations for any two of the four questions.

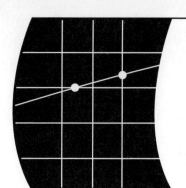

Chapter 2:
Algebra

2.1 THE LANGUAGE OF ALGEBRA

Any situation in which one or more numbers are unknown can be made into an algebra problem. When an algebra problem is presented in words, part of the task of solving the problem is to rewrite the information using algebraic expressions. *Algebraic expressions* contain numbers, variables, and symbols for the operations. *Algebraic equations* are statements containing two algebraic expressions joined with a sign of equality. *Algebraic inequalities* contain two algebraic expressions joined with a sign of inequality.

Key Words	Symbol	English and Algebra Translations
Signs of Operation		
sum, add, increase, more than, plus, increased by, greater, exceeded by, and	+	s increased by 10 $s + 10$ the sum of x and 7 $x + 7$
difference, subtract, take away, minus, decrease, fewer, less, less than, decreased by, diminished by	−	3 less than y $y - 3$ 45 fewer marbles than David $45 - D$
multiply, of, product, times	×	the product of 5 and t $5 \times t$ and $5t$ One-half the pumpkin weighs 3 pounds $\frac{1}{2}p = 3$
divide, quotient, into, for, per, divided by	÷	500 divided into 4 parts $500 \div 4$ Justin cut a 24-inch board into 8 pieces $24 \div 8$

Key Words	Symbol	English and Algebra Translations
Sign of Equality		
equals, is equivalent to, is the result of, is	$=$	Three times a number plus 2 is 20 $3x + 2 = 20$
Signs of Inequality		
is greater than, is more, has more	$>$	x is greater than 7 $x > 7$
is less than, is fewer, has fewer	$<$	Pauline and Blasé together have fewer books than Anthony $P + B < A$
is greater than or equal to, is at least, has at least	$\geq$	The party was at least 4 hours long $p \geq 4$
is less than or equal to, is at most, has at most	$\leq$	The theatre is at most 1.5 miles away $t \leq 1.5$
is not equal to, is not the same as, cannot equal, does not equal	$\neq$	Amanda is not 7 years old $A \neq 7$

Points to Remember

- Before you translate a problem situation into an algebraic expression, be sure you understand what the situation means.
- Define each variable you create with an equal sign.
- When there are two or more unknown quantities, you may need to represent only one of them with a letter variable. Try to express the other unknown quantities in terms of that letter if possible.
- Often, translation assumes that you know certain relationships about money, measurement, or time. If a relationship is not clear to you, you should try making a chart or table of the situation before translating it into an algebraic expression.

1. If x = Luke's age and $x + 6$ = Nancy's age in years, write an equation for each of the following statements:

   • The sum of Luke's and Nancy's age is less than 30 years

Solution:

$$x + (x + 6) < 30$$

   • Three times Luke's age equals twice Nancy's age.

Solution:

$$3x = 2(x + 6)$$

   • The difference between Nancy's age in 10 years and twice Luke's present age is 4 years.

Solution:

$$[(x + 6) + 10] - 2x = 4$$

2. When 8 is subtracted from 3 times a number, the result is 19. Which of the following equations represents this statement?

   A $8 - 3x = 19$
   B $3x - 8 = 19$
   C $3(x - 8) = 19$
   D $3(8 - x) = 19$

Solution:

Let x = the number.
Then "3 times a number" = $3x$.
"8 is subtracted from 3 times a number" = $3x - 8$.
"The result is" translates into an equal sign. Thus, $3x - 8 = 19$.

Answer: B

3. Albert has 20 coins, all nickels and dimes, that have a total value of $1.25. If n represents the number of nickels, which algebraic equation represents this situation?

   F $20n = 125$
   G $5n = 1.25$
   H $5n + 10(20 - n) = 125$
   J $5n + 10n - 20 = 125$

Solution:

Let the number of nickels = n.
Then the value of the nickels at five cents per nickel = $5n$.
Since Albert has 20 coins in all, the number of dimes he has is 20 minus the number nickels. Thus, the number of dimes = $20 - n$.
The value of the dimes at 10 cents per dime = $10(20 - n)$.
The total amount of money is the sum of the values of the nickels and the dimes. Thus, Albert's total = $5n + 10(20 - n)$. If the total value is $1.25, then $5n + 10(2 + n) = 125$ cents.

Answer: C

1. Eight years ago, Clyde was 7 years old. Which equation is true if C represents Clyde's age now?

    A $8 + C = 7$
    B $7 + C = 8$
    C $8 - 7 = C$
    D $C - 8 = 7$

2. Which of the following represents the total cost of x shirts bought at a cost of $(x + 5)$ dollars each?

    F $(x + 5)$ dollars   **H** $x(x + 5)$ dollars
    G $x + (x + 5)$ dollars   **J** $x^2 + 5$ dollars

3. If a batch of holiday cookies requires 2 cups of flower, how many cups of flour would be used in baking m batches of cookies?

    A $m + 3$ **C** $\dfrac{m}{3}$
    B $m - 3$ **D** $3m$

4. George is 15 years old. He is one-third as old as his father. Which equation is true if g represents George's father's age?

    F $3g = 15$ **H** $\dfrac{1}{3}g = 15$
    G $g + 3 = 15$ **J** $g - 3 = 15$

5. Which of the following is the correct translation of the following situation: Maria is at least 10 years older than Nadine?

    A $n > 2n - 10$ **C** $m \geq n + 10$
    B $n = m - 10$ **D** $2n < n + 10$

For questions 6 through 9, represent each situation with an algebraic equation.

6. A number squared, increased by 15, is the same as the square of 1 more than the number.

7. In 20 years, Tracy's age will be 5 years greater than twice her current age.

8. David worked 6 hours on Friday and $x + 2$ hours on Saturday at a constant rate of pay. He earned $92.

9. The quotient of p divided by r, decreased by the product of p and r, is 5.

10. Dominic has $12.50 in pennies, dimes, and half-dollars in his piggy bank. He has 5 times as many dimes as half-dollars and 5 times as many pennies as dimes. Answer the following.

    • If Dominic has h half-dollars, write an expression for the number of dimes and pennies he has.
    • Using these expressions, write an equation showing that the total value of Dominic's coins is $12.50.

2.2 ADDING AND SUBTRACTING ALGEBRAIC EXPRESSION

A *variable* is a letter used to represent a number. The value of a variable can change. A *term* is a number, a variable, or the product or quotient of a number and a variable. Recall from the previous section that an algebraic expression is made up of one or more terms.

Algebraic Expressions	Constant Terms
$6a$	7
$x + 4$	4π
a^2b	$\sqrt{2}$

The value of an expression involving a variable depends upon the value used for the variable.

When evaluating an expression be sure to follow the established algebraic *order of operations*.

- Perform any operation(s) inside grouping symbols.
- Simplify any terms with exponents.
- Multiply and divide in order from left to right.
- Add and subtract in order from left to right.

MODEL PROBLEMS

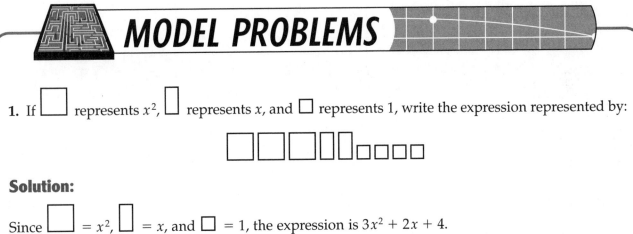

1. If ▢ represents x^2, ▯ represents x, and ▢ represents 1, write the expression represented by:

Solution:

Since ▢ $= x^2$, ▯ $= x$, and ▢ $= 1$, the expression is $3x^2 + 2x + 4$.

2. Evaluate $3a^2 + 4ab - b^2$ for $a = 2$ and $b = {}^-1$.

Solution:

$$3(2)^2 + 4(2)({}^-1) - ({}^-1)^2$$
$$3 \cdot 4 + ({}^-8) \quad - 1$$
$$12 - \quad 8 \quad - 1$$
$$4 \quad - 1 = 3$$

In a term that contains a variable, the numerical factor is called the *coefficient*.

coefficient ⟶ ⌐ ⌐ exponent
$$3x^2$$
└── base

An algebraic expression of exactly one term is called a *monomial*. Examples of monomials include 7, a, and $5x^2$.

If terms have exactly the same variables raised to the same powers, they are called *like terms*.

Like Terms
$5x^2$ and $\frac{1}{2}x^2$
$5a^2b$ and $6a^2b$

Not Like Terms
$3x^2$ and $3x^3$
$5ab$ and $6ac$

Since algebraic expressions themselves represent numbers, they can be added, subtracted, multiplied, and divided. When algebraic expressions are added or subtracted, they can be combined only if they have like terms.

To Add or Subtract Monomials With Like Terms

- Use the distributive property and the rules of signed numbers to add or subtract the coefficients of each term.
- Write this sum with the variable part from the terms.

MODEL PROBLEMS

1. Add $^-2x^3$ and $5x^3$.

Solution:

$$^-2x^3 + 5x^3 = (^-2 + 5)x^3 = 3x^3$$

2. Subtract $7mn^2$ from $4mn^2$.

Solution:

$$4mn^2 - 7mn^2 = (4 - 7)mn^2 = {}^-3mn^2$$

An algebraic expression of one or more unlike terms is a **polynomial**. **Binomials** are polynomials with *two* unlike terms: $7v + 9$ and $3x^2 - 8y$ are both binomials. **Trinomials** are polynomials with *three* unlike terms: $x^2 - 3x - 5$ and $3a^2bx - 5ax - 2ab$ are both trinomials.

A polynomial with one variable is said to be in **standard form** when it has no like terms and is written in order of descending exponents. For example, $4x + 9 - 5x^2 + 3x^3$ in standard form is $3x^3 - 5x^2 + 4x + 9$. When you are asked to *simplify* a polynomial, you should always write it in standard form.

To Add Polynomials

- Use the commutative property to arrange the terms so like terms are beside each other.
- Combine like terms.

 MODEL PROBLEM

Add $^-3x^2 + 4y$ and $5x^3 - 6x^2 - 3y$.

Solution:

$$(^-3x^2 + 4y) + (5x^3 - 6x^2 - 3y)$$
$$= {}^-3x^2 + 4y + 5x^3 - 6x^2 - 3y$$
$$= 5x^3 - 3x^2 - 6x^2 + 4y - 3y$$
$$= 5x^3 + (^-3 - 6)x^2 + (4 - 3)y$$
$$= 5x^3 - 9x^2 + 1y$$
$$= 5x^3 - 9x^2 + y$$

To Subtract Polynomials

- Change the sign of every term in the subtracted polynomial and remove parentheses.
- Combine like terms.

 MODEL PROBLEM

Subtract $9x^2 - 5x$ from $^-4x^2 - 8x$.

Solution:

First rewrite the problem to show the subtraction as $(^-4x^2 - 8x) - (9x^2 - 5x)$.
Change the signs in the subtracted polynomial and remove the parentheses.

$$(^-4x^2 - 8x) - (9x^2 - 5x)$$
$$= {}^-4x^2 - 8x - 9x^2 + 5x$$
$$= {}^-4x^2 - 9x^2 - 8x + 5x$$
$$= (^-4 - 9)x^2 + (^-8 + 5)x$$
$$= {}^-13x^2 - 3x$$

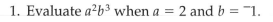

PRACTICE

1. Evaluate a^2b^3 when $a = 2$ and $b = {}^-1$.

   A 4   **B** ${}^-4$ **C** ${}^-32$ **D** ${}^-64$

2. Evaluate $5 + x(x + 2)$ when $x = 8$.

   F 71   **G** 85   **H** 122   **J** 130

3. If $n + 7$ is an even number, the next larger even number is:

   A $n + 5$ **C** $10n + 7$

   B $n + 9$ **D** $2n + 14$

4. Which of the following cannot be simplified?

   F $2a^2 + 5a^2$

   G $3a^2 - 3a$

   H $5a - 11a$

   J $16a^3 - 6a^3$

5. Which expression must be added to $2x - 4$ to produce a sum of 0?

   A 0   **C** $2x + 4$

   B $x + 2$ **D** ${}^-2x + 4$

6. The perimeter of the parallelogram is $6a + 8b$. Find the length of each of the other two sides.

   F $2a + 3b$

   G $2b + 3a$

   H $4a + 6b$

   J $3a + 4b$

7. Find the sum of ${}^-3x^2 - 4xy + 2y^2$ and ${}^-x^2 + 5xy - 8y^2$.

   A ${}^-2x^2 + xy - 6y^2$

   B ${}^-4x^2 + xy - 6y^2$

   C ${}^-4x^2 - 9xy - 6y^2$

   D ${}^-2x^2 - 9xy + 10y^2$

8. What is the result when ${}^-4x + 6$ is subtracted from $8x + 6$?

   F $12x + 12$ **H** $4x + 6$

   G $12x$ **J** $4x$

9. Write an equation to show that segment y is 5 units longer than 3 times the length of segment x.

   A $y = 15x$

   B $y = 3x + 5$

   C $x = 3y + 5$

   D $y = 3x - 5$

10. Find the value of A in the formula $A = \dfrac{1}{2}bh$ if $b = h = 5$.

11. A rectangle has dimensions $2x$ by $x + 3$. Write an expression for the perimeter of the rectangle. Combine any like terms.

12. Write the open sentence represented by the following situation. The congruent sides of an isosceles triangle have lengths that are each 5 inches greater than the length of the base. The perimeter is at most 31 inches.

13. Pat thinks that if $y = 5$, the expression ${}^-y^2$ and the expression $({}^-y)^2$ will result in the same value. Write an explanation to agree or disagree.

14. Is the expression for twice the sum of a number and 10 the same as the expression for the sum of twice a number and 10? Explain.

15. If a taxi ride costs d dollars a mile for the first 5 miles and $d + n$ dollars for each additional mile, write an expression that describes the cost, in dollars, to ride each of the following distances. Combine like terms in your answers.

   • 5 miles
   • 6 miles
   • 7 miles
   • 8 miles

2.3 MULTIPLYING ALGEBRAIC EXPRESSIONS

To Find the Product of Monomials

- Multiply the numerical coefficients using the rule of signs for multiplication.
- Multiply the variables of the same base by adding the exponents.
- Multiply these two products together.

 MODEL PROBLEM

Multiply $^-4a^2b^3$ and $3a^3b$.

Solution:

$$(^-4a^2b^3)\,(3a^3b)$$
$$= (^-4 \cdot 3)(a^2 \cdot a^3 \cdot b^3 \cdot b^1)$$
$$= {}^-12a^5b^4$$

To Find the Product of a Polynomial and a Monomial

- First use the distributive property to remove parentheses.
- Then multiply each term of the polynomial by the monomial separately.
- Simplify the product if possible.

 MODEL PROBLEMS

1. $^-6(2a^2 - 3a + 1)$

Solution:

$$= {}^-6(2a^2) + (^-6)(^-3a) + (^-6)(1)$$
$$= {}^-12a^2 + 18a - 6$$

2. $3a^2b(a^2 - 2ab - 3b^2)$

Solution:

$$= 3a^2b(a^2) + 3a^2b(^-2ab) + 3a^2b(^-3b^2)$$
$$= 3a^4b - 6a^3b^2 - 9a^2b^3$$

When we multiply polynomials, each term of one polynomial must multiply each term of the other polynomial. The distributive property is one method for multiplying polynomials.

To Use the Distributive Property for Multiplying Polynomials

- Distribute the first polynomial over the terms of the second.
- Solve as before.

 MODEL PROBLEMS

1. Multiply: $(x + 2)(x + 3)$

Solution:

$(x + 2)(x + 3)$

$= (x + 2)x + (x + 2)3$ Distribute $(x + 2)$ over x and 3.

$= x^2 + 2x + 3x + 6$ Distribute x over the first $(x + 2)$ and 3 over the second.

$= x^2 + 5x + 6$ Combine like terms.

2. $(2x - 3)(3x^2 - 5x + 4)$

Solution:

$(2x - 3)(3x^2 - 5x + 4)$

$= (2x - 3)3x^2 + (2x - 3)(^-5x) + (2x - 3)4$

$= 6x^3 - 9x^2 - 10x^2 + 15x + 8x - 12$

$= 6x^3 - 19x^2 + 23x - 12$

 **PRACTICE**

1. Find the product of $3x^2$ and $2x^3$.

     A $5x^5$ **C** $6x^5$

     B $5x^6$ **D** $6x^6$

2. Find the product: $2x^5y^2 \cdot 5xy^3z^2 \cdot 2yz$

     F $9x^6y^6z^3$ **H** $20x^5y^6z^2$

     G $20x^5y^6z^2$ **J** $20x^6y^6z^3$

3. Find the product: $(2x + 6)(x - 3)$

     A $2x^2 + 3x - 18$ **C** $2x^2 - 18$

     B $2x^2 + x - 18$ **D** $3x + 3$

4. Find the product: $(3a - 2)(5a - 5)$

     F $15a^2 - 31a - 10$ **H** $15a^2 - 5a + 10$

     G $15a^2 - 25a + 10$ **J** $8a^2 - 25a + 7$

5. Find the product of $2x^2y^3$ and $4x^2y^4$.

6. Find the product of $x(^-2x)^3$.

7. Simplify $a^3 - 5a^2 - a(3a + 3 - a^3)$.

8. Simplify $3(4x - 5) - (2x - 10)$.

Dividing Algebraic Expressions by a Monomial

To Divide a Monomial by Another Monomial

- Divide the numerical coefficients, using the law of signs for division.
- Find the quotient of the variables, using the laws of exponents.
- Multiply the two quotients.
- Check the answer by multiplying.

 MODEL PROBLEMS

1. $\dfrac{24x^5}{-3x^2}$

Solution:

$= \dfrac{24}{-3} \cdot \dfrac{x^5}{x^2} = \dfrac{8}{-1} \cdot x^{5-2} = {}^-8x^3$

Check: $({}^-3x^2) \times ({}^-8x^3) = 24x^5$

2. $\dfrac{{}^-8a^3b^2}{8a^3b}$

Solution:

$= \dfrac{{}^-8}{8} \cdot \dfrac{a^3}{a^3} \cdot \dfrac{b^2}{b} = ({}^-1)(1)b = {}^-b$

Check: $(8a^3b)({}^-b) = {}^-8a^3b^2$

To Divide a Polynomial by a Monomial

- Divide each term of the polynomial by the monomial, using the distributive property.
- Combine the quotients with correct signs.
- Check by multiplying.

 MODEL PROBLEMS

1. $\dfrac{6m^2 - m}{{}^-m}$

Solution:

$= \dfrac{6m^2}{{}^-m} + \left(\dfrac{{}^-m}{{}^-m}\right) = {}^-6m^{(2-1)} + 1 = {}^-6m + 1$

Check: ${}^-m({}^-6m + 1) = 6m^2 - m$

2. $\dfrac{9x^5 - 6x^3}{3x^2}$

Solution:

$= \dfrac{9x^5}{3x} + \left(\dfrac{{}^-6x^3}{3x^2}\right) = 3x^3 - 2x$

Check: $3x^2(3x^3 - 2x) = 9x^5 - 6x^3$

3. $\dfrac{4a^2x - 8ax + 12ax^2}{4ax}$

Solution:

$= \dfrac{4a^2x}{4ax} - \dfrac{8ax}{4ax} + \dfrac{12ax^2}{4ax} = a - 2 + 3x$

Check: $4ax(a - 2 + 3x) = 4a^2x - 8ax + 12ax^2$

PRACTICE

1. Divide: $\dfrac{x^4y^5z^2}{x^2y^3z}$

 A x^2y^2z C x^2yz^2

 B x^6y^8z D $x^2y^2z^2$

2. Divide: $\dfrac{^-0.08a^3x^2y^4}{^-0.2axy^2}$

 F $0.4a^2xy^2$ H $^-0.016a^2xy^2$

 G $0.4a^3x^2y^2$ J $^-4a^3x^2y^2$

3. Simplify: $\dfrac{6x^2 + 12x^3}{-6x^2}$

 A $1 - 2x$ C $^-x + 2x^2$

 B $^-1 - 2x$ D $2x - 1$

4. Simplify: $\dfrac{a^5x - 2a^4x^2 + a^3x^3}{a^2x}$

 F $a^5x - 2a^2x + a^3x^3$ H $a^3 - 2a^2x + ax^2$

 G $a^3x - 2a^2x^2 + ax^3$ J $a^2 - 2a^2x + ax$

For questions 5 through 10: Simplify the following expressions by dividing by the monomial or constant.

5. $\dfrac{a^4b^3c^7}{a^3c^4}$

6. $\dfrac{4a^2 - a}{^-a}$

7. $\dfrac{^-18r^4c^2}{^-3rc}$

8. $\dfrac{5x^4 + 3x^2}{x^2}$

9. $\dfrac{4a^2 + 3b^2 - c^2}{^-1}$

10. $\dfrac{9a^5b^3 - 27a^2b^2 + 6a^3b^5}{^-3ab^2}$

2.4   LITERAL EQUATIONS AND FORMULAS

Algebraic expressions have no specific value until values are substituted for each variable. Algebraic equations made of algebraic expressions cannot be called true or false until values are chosen from the domain for each variable.

The set of numbers from the domain that makes the equation true is called the **solution set** of the equation.

An equation with more than one variable is called a *literal equation*. For example, $x + y = r$ and $3m = 2n + 1$ are literal equations. A *formula* is a literal equation that expresses a rule about a real-world relationship. For instance, $d = rt$ is a formula comparing distance to rate and time.

To Find the Value of a Variable From a Literal Equation or Formulas

- Write the equation.
- Substitute the known values of the variables.
- Simplify and solve for the value of the remaining variable.
- State the answer with the correct label.

MODEL PROBLEMS

1. If a slug that has been traveling 1 inch per hour has covered a distance of 24 inches, how long has it been moving?

Solution:

$d = rt$	This relation is described by the formula $d = rt$.
24 in. $= (1 \text{ in.}/\text{h})t$	Substitute known values.
$t = \dfrac{24 \text{ in.}}{1 \text{ in.}/\text{h}}$	Solve for the variable t.
$t = 24$ hours or 1 day	Answer with the correct label.

2. Ann is enclosing a rectangular flower bed with a border. How many feet of border are needed if the flower bed measures 4 feet long by 3 feet wide?

Solution:

$P = 2l + 2w$	The relation is described by the formula $P = 2l + 2w$.
$P = 2(4 \text{ ft}) + 2(3 \text{ ft})$	Substitute known values.
$P = 14 \text{ ft}$	Answer with the correct label.

Answer: Ann needs 14 feet of border to enclose the flower bed.

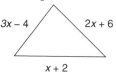
1. The centripetal force, F, of a rotating object equals the mass, m, multiplied by the square of the velocity, v, divided by the radius, r, of its path. This formula can be written as

   A $F = m + \left(\dfrac{v}{r}\right)^2$ **C** $F = \dfrac{m + v^2}{r}$

   B $F = \dfrac{(mv)^2}{r}$ **D** $F = \dfrac{mv^2}{r}$

2. To find the cost of two quarts of milk and three packages of cream cheese if each quart of milk costs $1.50 and each package of cream cheese costs $2.50, which formula would you use?

   F $C = m + c$, where $m = 1.5$ and $c = 2.5$
   G $C = 3m + 2c$, where $m = 1.5$ and $c = 2.5$
   H $C = 2m + 3c$, where $m = 1.5$ and $c = 2.5$
   J $C = 2m \cdot 3c$, where $m = 1.5$ and $c = 2.5$

3. If $S = \dfrac{rm - a}{r - 1}$, what is the value of S when $r = 3$, $m = 15$, and $a = 5$?

   A 10   **C** 20
   B 15   **D** 25

4. Find the number of miles traveled by Mrs. Smith if she drove 40 miles per hour for $\frac{3}{4}$ hour and 65 miles per hour for $3\frac{1}{2}$ hours.

   F 485 miles   **H** $257\frac{1}{2}$ miles

   G $332\frac{1}{2}$ miles   **J** $109\frac{1}{4}$ miles

5. Find the perimeter of a rectangle with length 56 centimeters and width 34 centimeters.

   A 44 cm   **C** 180 cm
   B 88 cm   **D** 476 cm

6. Leo is putting new tile on his bathroom floor. How many square feet of tile does he need if the floor measures 9 feet long and 6 feet wide?

   F 54 sq ft   **H** 27 sq ft
   G 30 sq ft   **J** 19 sq ft

7. The sides of a triangle are $x + 2$, $2x + 6$, and $3x - 4$. Find the perimeter of the triangle.

   ```
          3x – 4  /\  2x + 6
                 /  \
                /____\
                 x + 2
   ```

   A $P = 5x + 4$ **C** $P = 6x + 4$
   B $P = 6x - 12$ **D** $P = 5x - 12$

8. Julie needs to replace the carpet in her living room. If her living room measures 9 feet by 12 feet, find the cost of the carpet if carpet cost $9.85 per square yard.

   F $1,053.20   **H** $98.50
   G $118.20   **J** $88.50

9. Find the value of A if $A = \pi dh + \dfrac{1}{2}\pi d^2$ and $\pi = 3.14$, $h = 7$ centimeters, and $d = 10$ centimeters.

   A $A = 476.99$ cm²   **C** $A = 230.5$ cm²
   B $A = 376.8$ cm²   **D** $A = 219.8$ cm²

10. The area of a rectangle with length 5 yards is 375 square feet. Find the width of the rectangle.

    F 15 ft   **G** 25 ft   **H** 75 ft   **J** 175 ft

11. The formula for the volume of a sphere is $V = \dfrac{4}{3}\pi r^3$. Find the value of V in terms of π when $r = 3$ centimeters.

12. Write a formula for the cost C in dollars for renting a movie if the cost is $4 for the first 2 days and $1.50 for each additional day.

13. Sales tax is 5%. If the price paid for an item is P, write a formula that can be used to find N, the price of the item before tax.

14. A car rides at a constant rate of 60 miles per hour. How long will it take to travel 105 miles?

15. $C = 7N$ is a formula that can be used to find the cost, C, of any number of articles, N, that sell for $7 each. Answer the following.

    - How will the cost of 9 articles compare to the cost of 3 articles?
    - If N is doubled, what happens to C?

LINEAR EQUATIONS

An equation represents that two expressions are equal to each other.
  An equation is similar to a balanced scale.
  To determine the unknown weight in a balance:

- Remove (cancel) identical items from both sides of the scale.
- Determine a relationship between the remaining items.
- Substitute the value for the known quantity.
- Determine the weight of the unknown quantity.

MODEL PROBLEMS

Given the balances as shown, find the weight of one cube if each ball weighs 1 pound and the cubes are all the same weight.

1.

Solution:
- Remove two cubes and one ball from each side of the scale.
- One cube is balanced by three balls.
- Each ball weighs 1 pound.
- One cube weighs 3 pounds. **Answer**

2.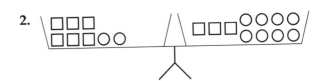

Solution:
- Remove three cubes and two balls from each side of the scale.
- Three cubes are balanced by six balls.
- Each ball weighs 1 pound.
- Three cubes weigh 6 pounds, and one cube weighs 2 pounds. **Answer**

The more traditional method of solving an equation involves use of mathematical properties.
  To solve an equation:

- Remove parentheses by multiplication. (Apply the Distributive Property.)
- Combine like terms in each member of the equation. Use addition or subtraction as indicated.
- Collect the terms containing the variable on one side and the number terms on the other side. Using the opposite operation of the one indicated (the inverse operation) will move a term from one side of the equation to the other.
- Rewrite the variable term with a coefficient of 1. Use the opposite operation of the division or multiplication indicated.

1. Solve for x: $6x = 2(x + 1) + 10$

Solution:

$$6x = 2(x + 1) + 10$$

$$6x = 2x + 2 + 10 \qquad \text{Remove parentheses.}$$

$$6x = 2x + 12 \qquad \text{Combine like terms.}$$

$$6x - 2x = 2x - 2x + 12 \qquad \begin{array}{l}\text{Collect the variable terms}\\ \text{on one side.}\end{array}$$

$$4x = 12$$

$$\frac{4x}{4} = \frac{12}{4} \qquad \begin{array}{l}\text{Rewrite the variable term}\\ \text{with a coefficient of 1.}\\ \text{Divide.}\end{array}$$

$$x = 3$$

2. Solve for y: $^-5y + 7 = ^-2(y - 5)$

Solution:

$$^-5y + 7 = ^-2(y - 5)$$

$$^-5y + 7 = ^-2y + 10 \qquad \begin{array}{l}\text{Remove parentheses.}\\ \text{No need to combine like terms.}\\ \text{Collect the variable terms on}\\ \text{one side}\end{array}$$

$$^-5y + 2y + 7 = ^-2y + 2y + 10$$

$$^-3y + 7 = 10$$

$$^-3y + 7 - 7 = 10 - 7 \qquad \begin{array}{l}\text{and the number terms on the}\\ \text{other side.}\end{array}$$

$$^-3y = 3$$

$$\frac{^-3y}{^-3} = \frac{3}{^-3} \qquad \begin{array}{l}\text{Rewrite the variable term with}\\ \text{a coefficient of 1. Divide.}\end{array}$$

$$y = ^-1$$

Solutions to some equations can be found by using a table or a graph.

Consider the equation $6(x + 1) = 15$. If you graph $6(x + 1) = y$ and locate the point on the graph where $y = 15$, the corresponding x-value of the ordered pair containing $y = 15$ would represent the solution to the equation.

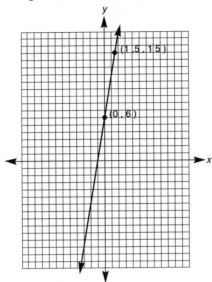

Another approach involves using a table of values. Look at the table given for $6(x + 1) = y$.

x	y
0	6
1	12
2	18

To solve $6(x + 1) = 15$, observe that 15 is midway between 12 and 18. Therefore, the value of x that satisfies the equation must be midway between 1 and 2, or 1.5.

 MODEL PROBLEM

Use a table to find the solution for the linear equation $3x + 4 = 6$.

Solution: Consider $3x + 4 = 6$ as $3x + 4 = y$ and generate a table of values.

x	y
0	4
1	7
2	10

Notice that $y = 6$ falls between 4 and 7. In fact it is $\frac{2}{3}$ of the way between 4 and 7. Therefore, the corresponding x value must be $\frac{2}{3}$ of the way between 0 and 1, or $\frac{2}{3}$.

Answer: $x = \frac{2}{3}$

1. Samantha's science book is twice the size of her math book. Together the two books have a total of 2,028 pages. How many pages are in her science book?

   A 676
   B 876
   C 1,014
   D 1,352

2. Andrew, Arthur, and Tommy share food expenses. Andrew pays $15.00 a month less than Tommy. Arthur pays twice as much as Andrew. If the monthly food bill is $420.00, how much does Tommy pay?

   F $158.33
   G $125.00
   H $116.25
   J $105.00

3. Which equation has NO integral solution?

   A $3x = 9$ **C** $3x = 2$
   B $16x = 32$ **D** $17x = 51$

4. Solve for c: $\dfrac{c}{6} + 14 = 38$

   F 4   **G** 144   **H** 214   **J** 312

5. Which of the following equations has a solution that is different from the others?

   A $x - 12 = 15$
   B $4x - 3(x + 2) = 11$
   C $2x - 1 = 33$
   D $3(x - 4) = 39$

6. Angela bought a bike for $6.00 less than one-fourth its original price. Angela paid $35.00 for the bike. What was the original price of the bike?

7. Eight times a number increased by 5 is equal to 89. What is the number?

8. Solve for x: $2(x + 1) - 4 = x + 3$

9. How do you know that the solution to the equation $3x = 251$ is NOT an integral value?

10. Given the balance shown, find the weight of each identical cube if each ball weighs 1 pound.

11. Solve for r:

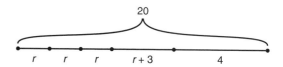

12. The temperature at High Point is 28°C and is dropping at the rate of 1.5° per hour. The temperature at Belmare is about 18°C and rising to 2° per hour. Answer the following.

    • Write an expression representing the temperature at each place after x hours.
    • Write an equation to represent that both cities are at the same temperature.
    • Solve the equation to find out how many hours (to the nearest tenth) it will take for the two cities to be at the same temperature.

INEQUALITIES

An inequality consists of two or more terms or expressions connected by an inequality sign.

The solution to an inequality is given as a solution set and can be represented on a number line.

The process of solving an inequality is very similar to the process of solving an equation. The major difference is if you are multiplying or dividing the inequality by a *negative number*, you must reverse the order of the inequality sign.

Note: A closed circle indicates the value is included in the solution set. An open circle indicates the value is excluded from the solution set.

MODEL PROBLEMS

1. Graph the inequality on the number line: $^-2 < x \leq 4$

Solution: The inequality is read "x is between $^-2$ and 4 with $^-2$ excluded and 4 included." On the number line the graph would be:

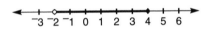

2. Solve for x: $^-4x + 4 \leq ^-16$

Solution:

$$^-4x + 4 \leq ^-16$$
$$^-4x + 4 - 4 \leq ^-16 - 4 \qquad \text{Add } ^-4.$$
$$^-4x \leq ^-20$$
$$\frac{^-4x}{^-4} \geq \frac{^-20}{^-4} \qquad \text{Divide by } ^-4; \text{ reverse inequality sign.}$$
$$x \geq 5$$

3. Write an inequality to describe the following situation and solve: Seven less than twice a number is greater than $^-3$. Find the number.

Solution:

$$2x - 7 > ^-3$$
$$2x > 4$$
$$x > 2$$

4. What is the value of x so that the sum of three consecutive integers is greater than 75?

Solution:

Let x = the first number.
$x + 1$ = the second number.
$x + 2$ = the third number.

$$x + (x + 1) + (x + 2) > 75$$
$$x + x + 1 + x + 2 > 75$$
$$3x + 3 > 75$$
$$\frac{3x}{3} > \frac{72}{3}$$
$$x > 24$$

Write the inequality.
Solve the inequality.

Divide each side by 3.

PRACTICE

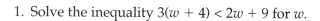

1. Solve the inequality $3(w + 4) < 2w + 9$ for w.

   A $w < {}^-21$ **C** $w < {}^-3$
   B $w > {}^-3$ **D** $w > 21$

2. Which number line shows the graph of ${}^-3 \leq x < 4$?

   F ![number line -3 to 5]
   G ![number line -3 to 5]
   H ![number line -3 to 5]
   J ![number line -3 to 5]

3. Three-fourths of a number increased by three is greater than or equal to 9. What is the number?

   A $x \leq {}^-8$ **C** $x > 8$
   B $x \geq 8$ **D** $x \geq 48$

4. Ten years from now, Lawrence will be more than twice as old as he is now. Which inequality below represents his age?

   F $2x + x > 10$ **H** $x - 10 > 2x$
   G $x + 10 > 2x$ **J** $10 + 2x > x$

5. Peter receives a salary of $250.00 a week plus a commission of $50.00 on each computer he sells. How many computers must he sell to make at least $500.00 a week?

   A 4   **B** 5   **C** 6   **D** 7

6. What is the solution of the inequality $2x + 5 \geq \frac{2}{3}x - 1$?

   F $x \geq -\frac{9}{2}$ **H** $x \geq 3$
   G $x \geq {}^-3$ **J** $x \geq \frac{9}{2}$

7. Solve for x: ${}^-5x + 3 \geq 28$.

8. Solve $2(x + 4) - 4x < 5x + 8$.

9. Write an inequality to describe the following situation and solve:

   Nine more than half a number is at most ${}^-8$.

10. The perimeter of a rectangular pool is at least 512 feet. Write an inequality that represents the perimeter of the pool.

    (4x + 8) feet

    (4x) feet

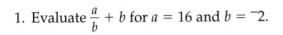

1. Evaluate $\frac{a}{b} + b$ for $a = 16$ and $b = {}^-2$.

    A 6   **B** $^-6$ **C** $^-10$ **D** $^-16$

2. The inequality $^-3x > 12$ is equivalent to which of the following?

    F $x < {}^-4$ **H** $x < 4$

    G $x > {}^-4$ **J** $x > 4$

3. Solve this inequality: $3(x - 1) - 7 < x - 3$

    A $x < 0.5$ **C** $x < 3.5$

    B $x < 2.5$ **D** $x < 6.5$

4. Which of these expressions have been combined correctly?

    I. $3x^2 + 5x + 9x^2 - 4x = 12x^2 + 1$

    II. $5ab + 3c^2 - 2ab + 8c^2 = 3ab + 11c^2$

    III. $8p^3 + 8p^2 + 8p + 8 = 8p^3 + 8p^2 + 8p + 8$

    F I and II only

    G I and III only

    H II and III only

    J I, II, and III

5. A price p is increased 10%. Which of the following is NOT a representation for the new price?

    A $p + 0.1p$ **C** $1.1p$

    B $110\% \cdot p$ **D** $0.1p$

6. If the area of a trapezoid $= \frac{1}{2}h(b_1 + b_2)$, which of the following expressions represents the area of the trapezoid shown?

    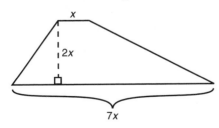

    F $6x^2$ **G** $8x^2$ **H** $10x^2$ **J** $16x^2$

7. Within the set of integers, which of the following represents the solution of the inequality

    $$4x + 1 < {}^-9$$

    A $\{^-1, 0, 1, 2, 3, \ldots\}$

    B $\{^-2, ^-1, 0, 1, 2, 3, \ldots\}$

    C $\{\ldots, ^-5, ^-4, ^-3\}$

    D $\{\ldots, ^-5, ^-4, ^-3, ^-2\}$

8. Which of the following sentences does the equation $5n - 3 = n + 11$ correctly represent?

    F 3 less than 5 times a number is 11.

    G 5 times 3 less than a number is 11 more than the number.

    H 3 more than 5 times a number is 11 more than the number.

    J 3 less than 5 times a number is 11 more than the number.

9. Which of the following represents the situation described?

    Joyce had $950 in her savings account. She withdrew the same amount each month for 5 months. After depositing $100 in her account, the balance was $908. How much money did she withdraw each month?

    A $950 - 5x = 908 + 100$

    B $950 + 5x - 100 = 908$

    C $950 - 5x + 100 = 908$

    D $950 - 5x - 100 = 908$

10. Write an equation to describe the situation. A car is rented for $15 a day plus $0.20 a mile. Martin paid $59.40 for a one-day rental.

    F $0.20x = \$59.40$

    G $0.20x - 15 = \$59.40$

    H $0.20x + 15 = \$59.40$

    J $0.20x + 15 + \$59.40$

11. Which inequality matches the situation? Take a number, add 3, multiply by 3, and subtract twice the original number. The result is greater than 5.

   A $3x + 3 > 5 - 2x$
   B $3x + 3 - 2x > 5$
   C $3(x + 3) - 2x > 5$
   D $9x - 2x > 5$

12. Select the inequality that describes the situation. Luis has \$22. He works for 5 days, receiving the same pay for each day. Then he will have no more than \$100.

   F $5x + 22 \geq 100$ **H** $22 - 5x \leq 100$
   G $5(x + 22) \leq 100$ **J** $5x + 22 \leq 100$

13. Which of these sequences of steps transforms the equation $3(x + 4) = 18$ into the equation $x = 2$?

   A Distribute the 3, subtract 4 from both sides, divide both sides by 3.
   B Distribute the 3, subtract 12 from both sides, divide both sides by 3.
   C Distribute the 3, subtract 12 from both sides, divide both sides by $\frac{1}{3}$.
   D Distribute the 3, divide both sides by 3, subtract 12.

14. For these equations, determine which ones have the same solution:

   I. $4x = 32$ II. $\frac{1}{4}x = \frac{1}{32}$ III. $40x = 320$

   F I and II only   **H** II and III only
   G I and III only   **J** I, II, and III

15. In which pair of equations are the two equations NOT equivalent?

   A $\dfrac{x}{5} = 3$
   $5 \cdot \dfrac{x}{5} = 3 \cdot 5$

   B $k + 14 = 8$
   $k + 14 - 14 = 8 - 14$

   C $6x = 21$
   $\dfrac{1}{6} \cdot 6x = \dfrac{1}{6} \cdot 21$

   D $3k - 4 = 11$
   $3k - 4 + 4 = 11 - 4$

16. Perform the indicated operation for the following:

   - $a^3b + 5a^3b$
   - $(5a - 3b) + (6a^2b + 7b)$
   - $(3a^3 + 4b^2 - c) + (2a^3 - 3b^2 - 3c)$
   - $(6x + 3) - (3x - 7)$
   - $(5x^2 - x + 7) - (3x^2 - 3x + 5)$
   - $(3x^2y^3)(5xy^6)$

17. Divide:

   - $\dfrac{a^3b^2cd}{bd}$
   - $\dfrac{36q + 20q^2}{4}$
   - $\dfrac{6s + 18s^2}{3s}$

18. Write an expression for the perimeter of the rectangle shown below.

   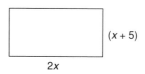

19. A parking garage charges \$2.00 for the first hour and \$1.25 for each additional hour of parking. The parking fees are given by the formula:

   $$F = 2.00 + 1.25(h - 1)$$

   where h is the number of hours and F is the total fee. What value completes the table showing parking fees?

h	1	2	4	...	10
F	2.00	3.25	5.75	...	?

20. Solve for a.

   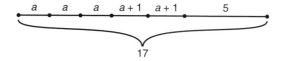

21. If the sum of four consecutive even integers is less than 250, what is the greatest possible value for one of these even integers? Explain your procedure.

22. This table shows a linear relationship between x and y.

x	y
1	3
2	5
3	7
4	9

Based on the indicated relationship:

- Provide three additional pairs of values in the table.
- Graph the relationship on a coordinate grid.
- Express the relationship between x and y as an equation.

23. For the following number puzzle, explain why the answer will always be 3.

> Start with a number. Multiply it by 4. Add 6, divide by 2, and subtract twice your original number.

24. A train leaves the town of Monroe and heads for the town of Jackson 200 miles away. The train travels at the speed of 40 mph. Answer the following.

- If t represents the number of hours since the train left Monroe, write an expression to represent how far the train must still travel to reach Jackson.
- If the train has been traveling for more than three hours, how far is the train from Jackson?
- For what range of time will the train be between 30 and 100 miles from Jackson?

Cumulative Assessment

For Chapters 1 and 2

1. Which of the following would represent all the real numbers at least 7 units away from ⁻3 on the number line?

   A $|x| \geq 7$
   B $|x + 3| \geq 7$
   C $|x - 3| \geq 7$
   D $|x + 7| \geq {}^-3$

2. Which of the following sets contains the numbers $\frac{5}{8}$, π, 100, ⁻4.75?

   F Integers
   G Rational numbers
   H Real numbers
   J Irrational numbers

3. A college team sweatshirt has a wholesale price of $30.00. The Sports Exchange applies a 20% markup on the wholesale price to obtain the retail price. During a sale, the same sweatshirt is priced at 15% off the retail price. What is the sale price?

   A $20.40   C $31.50
   B $30.60   D $36.00

4. Which of the numbers below has all the following characteristics?

   - It is a multiple of 9.
   - It is a factor of 144.
   - It is a perfect square.

   F 18   G 36   H 49   J 72

5. How many two-digits numbers have all of the following characteristics?

    I. The number is a multiple of 16.
    II. The number is a factor of 144.
    III. The number is divisible by 3.

A 0   **B** 1   **C** 2   **D** 3

6. Which of the following does NOT show a 10% increase?

    F 100 to 110
    G 50 to 60
    H 10 to 11
    J $\frac{1}{10}$ to $\frac{11}{100}$

7. Every four days, 180 cars come through the assembly line. At this rate, how many cars come through in 7 days?

    A 45
    B 315
    C 720
    D 1,260

8. A mail-order company sells wrapping paper for $3.75 a roll. Find the cost of an order of 8 rolls including tax and shipping. Tax is charged at the rate of 6% and is charged only on the purchase, not the shipping.

Shipping Costs	
Cost of Paper (with tax)	**Add**
less than $10.00	$0.55
$10.01–20.00	$1.00
$20.01–30.00	$1.75
over $30.00	$2.25

    F $33.55
    G $33.66
    H $34.05
    J $36.46

9. Which of the following does not describe the expression $4a + 3$?

    A three more than four times a number
    B four times the sum of a number and three
    C four times a number, increased by three
    D the sum of four times a number and three

10. Which expression represents the total amount of money in n nickels and d dimes?

    F $n + d$
    G $0.50n + 0.10d$
    H $0.05n + 0.10d$
    J nd

11. In one subdivision, a single-story house must be at least 1,500 square feet and no more than 2,000 square feet in area. A rectangular house is 35 feet wide. How long can it be?

    A $1,500 \le 35l \le 2,000$
    B $1,500 < 35l < 2,000$
    C $1,500 \le 2l + 2(35) \le 2,000$
    D $1,500 < 2l + 2(35) < 2,000$

12. Write two different algebraic expressions to find the area of the given rectangle.

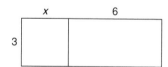

13. The scale on a map is $\frac{1}{2}$ inch = 65 miles. How far apart are two cities that are $6\frac{1}{2}$ inches apart on the map?

14. Matt borrowed $75 from Simon and started repaying the loan at the rate of $10 per week. In how many weeks will Matt's debt be less than $20?

15. A small banana has seven calories more than three times the calories in one serving (1 cup) of green beans. A small banana has 88 calories. What is the number of calories in a serving of green beans?

16. As a back-to-school incentive on Wednesdays, Supply Warehouse plans to give every fifteenth customer a free pen and every twenty-fifth customer a free notebook. On a particular Wednesday, Supply Warehouse had 300 customers. Answer the following.

    - How many free pens were given away on that Wednesday?
    - How many free notebooks were given away on that Wednesday?
    - Did any customers receive a free pen and a free notebook? If so, how many customers?
    - If pens sell for 79¢ and notebooks sell for $1.19, how much did the Supply Warehouse lose in income by giving away these items? Use mathematics to justify your answer.

17. The formula for the volume of a rectangular solid is

    $$V = lwh$$

    Answer the following.
    - What happens to the volume of a rectangular solid of the length is increased by 10%, the width is increased by 10%, and the height is also increased by 10%?
    - Suppose you want the volume of a second rectangular solid to be double the volume of the original solid. If each dimension of the original solid is to be increased by the same percent, what does this percent (to the nearest tenth of a percent) have to be?
    - In changing the dimensions of a rectangular solid, the length and width are each increased by 10%. The height is decreased by 20%. Marie says that the result is that the volume remains the same. Linda says that the volume is decreased by a very slight percent. Who is correct? Explain.

18. A student's score on a science test was determined by multiplying the number of correct answers C by 3.5, then subtracting the number of incorrect answers, W. Answer the following.

    - Write a formula for a student's score S.
    - Jason had 24 correct answers and 6 incorrect answers. What was his score?
    - Wilson had 28 correct answers and 2 incorrect answers. What was his score?

19. Popcorn is sold at a carnival for $2.50 per bag and candy apples are sold for $1.50 per apple. An inventory for last week showed that the number of bags of popcorn sold was four times the number of apples. The total amount collected for the two snacks was at least $500. What was the least possible number of bags of popcorn sold?

20. Jack and Bob are twins. Jack is trying to save money at a weekly rate to have the same amount of money as Bob. Bob has $310 saved but has needed to withdraw $20 per week to help meet his expenses. Jack has $100 to start and adds $10 per week to the amount. Answer the following.

    - Write an expression that represents the amount of money Jack will have after x weeks.
    - Write an expression that represents the amount of money Bob will have after x weeks.
    - At this rate how many weeks will it take until Jack and Bob have the same amount of money?

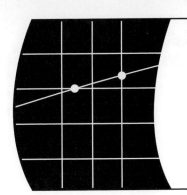

Chapter 3:
Data Analysis, Probability, and Statistics

3.1 — PROBABILITY OF SIMPLE EVENTS

The *probability* of an event is the ratio of the number of favorable outcomes to the total number of possible outcomes:

$$\text{probability} = \frac{\text{number of favorable outcomes}}{\text{total number of possible outcomes}}$$

The probability of an event can be expressed as a fraction, decimal, or percent with a value greater than or equal to zero and less than or equal to one. ($0 \le P \le 1$)

If $P(A) = 0$, then it is impossible for A to occur.

If $P(A) = 1$, then it is certain the event will occur.

A standard die is rolled. Find each of the following:

- the probability of rolling a 5
- the probability of rolling an even number
- the probability of rolling a number less than 3
- the probability of rolling a number greater than 7
- the probability of rolling a number less than 7

Solution: With the sample space consisting of 1, 2, 3, 4, 5, 6, the simple probabilities can be determined by applying the definition of probability.

- $P(5) = \dfrac{1}{6}$ (since 5 is the only favorable outcome)

- $P(\text{even}) = \dfrac{3}{6}$ (since 2, 4, and 6 are favorable outcomes)

- $P(< 3) = \dfrac{2}{6}$ (since 1 and 2 are favorable outcomes)

- $P(> 7) = 0$ (since there are no favorable outcomes)

- $P(< 7) = \dfrac{6}{6} = 1$ (since all outcomes are favorable)

Experimental and Theoretical Probabilities

Experimental probability results from conducting an experiment, making observations, or performing a simulation. For example, if you toss a coin 50 times and obtain 30 heads, the experimental probability of obtaining heads would be $\dfrac{30}{50}$ or $\dfrac{3}{5}$. Each time you toss the coin 50 times, the experimental probability of heads may vary.

In contrast with experimental probability, *theoretical probability* represents what you would expect from the "theory" or description of the situation. When we say that the probability of obtaining heads on the toss of a coin is $\dfrac{1}{2}$ or 50%, or the probability of obtaining an ace is $\dfrac{4}{52}$ or $\dfrac{1}{13}$, we are giving the theoretical probability.

1.

| Girls in Families of Four Children ||
Number of Girls	Frequency
0	10
1	15
2	49
3	19
4	7

The above table shows the results of data gathering on the number of girls in 100 families with four children. Answer the following:

- Based on the data, what is the experimental probability that exactly two children will be girls?
- Explain why your answer would most likely be different if you collected data from another group of 100 families consisting of four children.

Solution:

- From the information in the table, the experimental probability is $\frac{49}{100}$.

- The probabilities are based on the frequencies. As the data are gathered, it is not likely that you would get the same frequencies.

2. What is the theoretical probability of having exactly two girls in a family of four children?

Solution:

The sample space shows a total of 16 possibilities for combinations of boys and girls in a family with four children:

BBBB	BGBB	GGGG	GBGG
BBBG	BGBG	GGGB	GBGB
BBGB	BGGB	GGBG	GBBG
BBGG	BGGG	GGBB	GBBB

Since 6 of the sequences above represent exactly two girls (and two boys), the theoretical probability is $\frac{6}{16}$ or $\frac{3}{8}$ or 37.5%.

3. An appliance manufacturer selected 1,000 toasters at random. Of these, 4 were found to be defective. Answer the following.

- What is the probability of a toaster being defective?
- In a production run of 7,500 toasters, how many could be expected to have defects?

Solution:

- $P(\text{defective}) = \dfrac{\text{number of defective in sample}}{\text{total number in sample}} = \dfrac{4}{1,000} = .004$

- Expected number defective = $P(\text{defective}) \times$ number of items

  = .004(7,500)

  = 30

About 30 of the 7,500 toasters could be expected to have defects.

1. Which of the following cannot be the answer to a probability question?

   A 0   **B** 30%   **C** $\frac{11}{10}$ **D** $\frac{10}{11}$

2. You flip a fair coin. The first eight flips come up heads. What is the probability that the ninth flip of the coin will be a tail?

   F $\frac{1}{2}$ **G** 1   **H** $\frac{8}{9}$ **J** $\frac{1}{9}$

3. Consider the following events:

   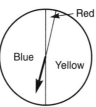

   I. Obtaining a sum of 2 in rolling two dice

   II. Obtaining 5 heads when tossing five coins

   III. Obtaining a red with one spin of the spinner shown

   Arrange the events in order from LEAST probable to MOST probable.

   A III, II, I
   B I, II, III
   C I, III, II
   D II, I, III

4. Two events, *A* and *B*, are considered **complementary** if $P(B) = 1 - P(A)$. For example, in tossing a coin, $P(\text{heads}) = \frac{1}{2}$ and $P(\text{tails}) = \frac{1}{2}$, which is equal to $1 - P(\text{heads})$. Which of the following would NOT represent complementary events?

   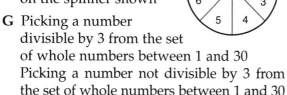

   F Spinning an odd number on the spinner shown
   Spinning an even number on the spinner shown

   G Picking a number divisible by 3 from the set of whole numbers between 1 and 30
   Picking a number not divisible by 3 from the set of whole numbers between 1 and 30

   H Obtaining a sum less than 7 when tossing two dice
   Obtaining a sum greater than 7 when tossing two dice

   J Picking a red card from a regular deck of cards
   Picking a black card from a regular deck of cards

5. A manufacturer randomly selected 5,000 computer chips and found that 85 were defective. In a production run of 100,000 chips, about how many can be expected not to be defective?

   A 1,700
   B 4,250
   C 24,575
   D 98,300

6. A group of students were asked to name their favorite weekday. The results are shown in the table below.

Favorite Weekday	
Monday	4
Tuesday	11
Wednesday	12
Thursday	15
Friday	28

   If 500 students were asked to name their favorite weekday, how many would be expected to say Friday?

   F 120
   G 135
   H 200
   J 280

7. For the spinner shown, the probability of landing on each color is $\frac{1}{4}$ or 25%.

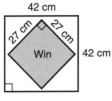

A different spinner has 3 sectors each with a different color (red, green, or yellow). If the ratio $P(\text{red}) : P(\text{green}) : P(\text{yellow})$ is $1 : 4 : 7$, draw the resulting spinner. Show your work and use a protractor.

8. A coin-toss game at a carnival has a board as shown. To win, the coin must land in the shaded area. What is the probability of winning the game, expressed to the nearest percent?

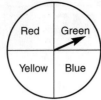

9. A dice game is played by two students using a pair of dice.

Player 1 gets a point if the product of the numbers rolled on the dice is even.

Player 2 gets a point if the product of the numbers rolled on the dice is odd.

The player with more points after 20 rounds wins.

Is the game, as outlined, fair or not? Explain.

10. Mary rolled a die 600 times. The results are shown below.

odd 252   even 348

Calculate the experimental probability for rolling odd as shown by the results given. Determine the theoretical probability for rolling an odd number on a die. Compare the experimental and theoretical probabilities. What could Mary have done to see if the experimental results would come closer to the theoretical results?

3.2 PROBABILITY OF COMPOUND EVENTS

Compound events consist of two or more events. If the outcome of one event does not affect the outcome of the other event, the events are *independent*.

For two independent events,

$$P(A \text{ and } B) = P(A) \cdot P(B)$$

If the outcome of one event affects the outcome of the other event, the events are *dependent*.

For two dependent events,

$$P(A \text{ and } B) = P(A) \cdot P(B \text{ after } A \text{ occurs})$$

1. Suppose a number cube is rolled twice. What is the probability that an odd number will occur both times?

Solution: Since the first and second rolls of the number cube are independent of each other, P(rolling 2 odd numbers) = P(first roll odd) · P(second roll odd)

outcomes: 1, 2, 3, 4, 5, 6   total 6

odd numbers: 1, 3, 5   total 3

$P(\text{odd}) = \dfrac{3}{6} = \dfrac{1}{2}$

$P(\text{rolling 2 odd numbers}) = \dfrac{1}{2} \cdot \dfrac{1}{2} = \dfrac{1}{4}$

2. A jar contains 3 red balls, 2 white balls, and 1 green ball. What is the probability of picking two white balls if the first ball is not replaced?

Solution:

$P(\text{first white}) = \dfrac{2}{6} = \dfrac{1}{3}$

Since the first ball selected was white and not replaced,

$P(\text{second white}) = \dfrac{1}{5}$

$P(\text{two whites}) = \dfrac{1}{3} \cdot \dfrac{1}{5} = \dfrac{1}{15}$

Probability of *A* or *B*

Sometimes you want to find the probability that either of two events will occur. This calculation depends on whether or not the events are mutually exclusive, that is, events that cannot occur at the same time.

For mutually exclusive events,

$$P(A \text{ or } B) = P(A) + P(B)$$

If the events are not mutually exclusive because it is possible for both to occur at the same time, the probability of *A* or *B* requires you to subtract the $P(A \text{ and } B)$ from the sum of $P(A) + P(B)$, because of the overlapping components of the sample space.

For non–mutually exclusive events,

$$P(A \text{ or } B) = P(A) + P(B) - P(A \text{ and } B)$$

For the spinner shown, find the following probabilities:

- P(a 2 or a 5)
- P(a multiple of 2 or a multiple of 3)

Solution:

- Since obtaining a 2 and obtaining a 5 are mutually exclusive, P(a 2 or a 5) $= P(2) + P(5) =$ $\frac{1}{8} + \frac{1}{8} = \frac{2}{8} = \frac{1}{4}$
- Since there is an overlapping condition, P(mult. of 2 or mult. of 3) $= P$(mult. of 2) $+ P$(mult. of 3) $- P$(mult. 2 and 3) $= \frac{4}{8} + \frac{2}{8} - \frac{1}{8} = \frac{5}{8}$

PRACTICE

1. A coin is tossed and a die with numbers 1–6 is rolled. What is P(heads and 3)?

   A $\frac{1}{12}$ **B** $\frac{1}{4}$ **C** $\frac{1}{3}$ **D** $\frac{2}{3}$

2. Two cards are selected from a deck of cards numbered 1 through 10. Once a card is selected it is not replaced. What is P(two even numbers)?

   F $\frac{1}{4}$ **G** $\frac{2}{9}$ **H** $\frac{1}{2}$ **J** 1

3. Which of the following is NOT an example of independent events?

   A Rolling a die and spinning a spinner
   B Tossing a coin two times
   C Picking two cards from a deck with replacement of first card
   D Selecting two marbles one at a time without replacement

4. A club has 25 members, 20 boys and 5 girls. Two members are selected at random to serve as president and vice president. What is the probability that both will be girls?

   F $\frac{1}{5}$ **G** $\frac{1}{25}$ **H** $\frac{1}{30}$ **J** $\frac{1}{4}$

5. One marble is randomly drawn and then replaced from a jar containing two white marbles and one black marble. A second marble is drawn. What is the probability of drawing a white and then a black?

   A $\frac{1}{3}$ **B** $\frac{2}{9}$ **C** $\frac{3}{8}$ **D** $\frac{1}{6}$

6. Maria rolls a pair of dice. What is the probability that she obtains a sum that is either a multiple of 3 OR a multiple of 4?

   F $\frac{5}{9}$ **G** $\frac{7}{12}$ **H** $\frac{1}{36}$ **J** $\frac{7}{36}$

7. Greg rolls a pair of dice. What is the probability that he obtains a sum of 2 OR 12?

8. Jack never pairs his socks after doing laundry. He just throws the socks into the drawer randomly. If the drawer contains 14 white socks and 12 grey socks, what is the probability he will select a pair of grey socks when selecting two socks at random? Give your answer as a decimal rounded to the nearest thousandth.

9. Find the probability of spinning red AND even given the spinners pictured.

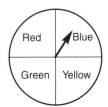 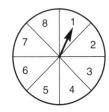

10. A basketball player is given two free throws for a foul committed against him. During the season, he has made 36 out of 50 free throws attempted. Using this experimental probability, find the probability of each event as a percent.

- Making both free throws
- Making neither free throw
- Making one free throw

11. Events A and B are independent. The probability of event A occurring is $\frac{3}{5}$ and the probability of event B not occurring is $\frac{2}{3}$. What is $P(A \text{ and } B)$?

12. Suppose E and F are independent events. The probability that event E will occur is .7 and the probability that event F will occur is .6.

- Find the probability of E and F both occurring.
- Explain why the answer should be less than each of the individual probabilities.
- Suppose E and F are independent events with the probability of E being p and the probability of F being q. If $P(E \text{ and } F) = .36$ and $P(E) \neq P(F)$, find a pair of possible values for p and q.

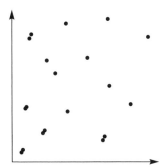

3.3 RELATIONSHIPS INVOLVING DATA

A *scatter plot* is a graph used to show a relationship or *correlation* between sets of data. In a scatter plot, we plot the data as ordered pairs, represented by unconnected points. The pattern of the data points shows the correlation, if any, between the two data sets. If most of the data points are clustered together along an imaginary line, the two data sets are correlated.

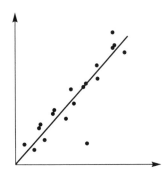 

Positive Correlation
both sets of data
increase together

Negative Correlation
one set of data
decreases as the
other set increases

No Correlation
the data sets are
not related

A *line of best fit* or *trend line* can be drawn where approximately half of the points are on each side of the line. If the line slopes upward, there exists a positive correlation. If the line slopes downward, there exists a negative correlation.

Outliers are points that lie far from the overall linear pattern.

Determining an Equation for a Line of Best Fit

The graph below shows the heights and shoe sizes for a group of males.

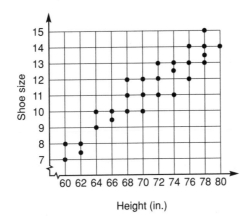

To determine an equation for a line of best fit, first sketch a line of best fit by drawing a line on the graph so that approximately half of the points are on each side of the line. In the graph above, the line of best fit can go through (62, 8) and (72, 12).

The slope of the line is $\frac{(12-8)}{(72-62)}$, which is equal to $\frac{4}{10}$ or $\frac{2}{5}$. The positive slope indicates that as the height increases, the shoe size increases. Specifically, the slope or the rate shows that the shoe size increases by 2 whenever the height increases by 5.

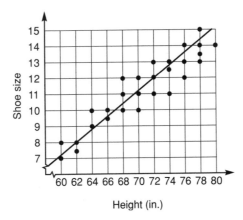

The line of best fit has the equation $y = \frac{2}{5}x - 16.8$. This equation can be used to predict the shoe size, y, given the height, x. For example, using the equation for the line of best fit to predict the shoe size of a male who is 71 inches tall, the shoe size is close to 11.5.

1. Plot the data given in the table on a graph and draw the line of best fit. Find the equation of the line of best fit. Does the graph show a positive or a negative correlation?

Height (in.)	60	62	63	65	68	69	70	70	72	74	75	75
Weight (lb)	120	122	125	130	132	142	158	147	150	152	160	156

Solution:

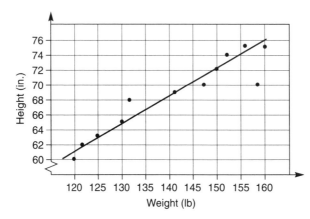

The line of best fit can be drawn going through the points (142, 69) and (150, 72). The slope of the line is $\dfrac{(72 - 69)}{(150 - 142)} = \dfrac{3}{8}$. The line of best fit has the equation $y = \dfrac{3}{8}x + 15.75$.

Answer: The equation of the line of best fit is $y = \dfrac{3}{8}x + 15.75$. The slope of the line is positive, which refers to a positive correlation.

2. Describe the correlation that would exist in each of the following:

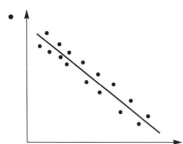

- Hours worked and earnings

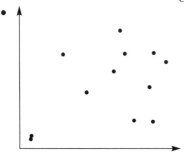

Solution:

- The scatter plot suggests a line that slopes downward to the right. The two data sets would have a negative correlation.
- You would expect to earn more if you worked more hours. Therefore, a positive correlation exists.
- The points are very spread out. There appears to be no correlation.

To construct a Scatter Plot on the Graphing Calculator

Note: The graphing calculator keystrokes are for the TI-83Plus calculator.

- Enter the data values for the independent variable in L_1.
- Enter the data values for the dependent variable in L_2.
- Check that there is the same number of values in both lists.
- Press [2nd] [Y=]
- Press [1]. The cursor should be over On. Press [ENTER] to turn STAT PLOT 1 on.
- Using the arrows and cursor, make sure the first graph type is selected, L_1 and L_2 are the lists to be graphed (unless your data is in other lists) and the mark is ▫.
- Adjust the window so all the values will appear on the graph. The best window is usually achieved by pressing [ZOOM] and selecting 9:ZoomStat

Using the Graphing Calculator to Construct the Line of Best Fit

When we use the calculator to construct the line of best fit, the calculator can also be set to return a *correlation coefficient,* which is a measure of how well the data fits the line. Before using the calculator to construct the line, we set the calculator to show the correlation coefficient by turning Diagnostics On; follow the steps listed below.

- Press [2nd] [0] to get into the CATALOG menu.
- Press [▼] to DiagnosticsOn
- Press [ENTER]
- Press [ENTER] again

The slope of the line will depend on whether the correlation is positive or negative. The "goodness of fit" is determined by the strength of the correlation. Enter the data into the calculator as two lists. Press [STAT], [▶] to CALC, press [4] to select 4:LinReg(ax+b). The home screen shows LinReg(ax+b) and a blinking cursor. Press [2nd] [1] [,] [2nd] [2], to insert L_1 and L_2, then press [,] [VARS] [▶] to Y-VARS, press [1] to select 1:Function, press [1], for Y_1, and press [ENTER].

The screen shows an equation for the line of best fit, displayed as $y = ax + b$. The value a is the slope. The value b is the y-intercept. The value r is the *correlation coefficient*, where $^-1 \leq r \leq 1$. If r is positive, the correlation is positive. Likewise, if r is negative, the correlation is negative.

- Strong positive or strong negative correlation: $|r| \geq 0.8$
- Moderate positive or moderate negative correlation: $0.5 < |r| < 0.8$
- Weak Correlation: $|r| \leq 0.5$

Press $\boxed{\text{Y=}}$ and the formula for the line is assigned to Y_1 and can be graphed along with the scatter plot by pressing $\boxed{\text{GRAPH}}$.

Correlation and Causation

We should be careful when we interpret scatter plots. In cases where we see strong correlation, we sometimes assume that the variable values in the X list cause the values in the Y list. Just because two variables are strongly correlated, we cannot assume that one causes the other. A correlation may be a mere coincidence. For example, if we find a high correlation between sales of a particular product and arrests for a particular crime, we cannot say that one causes the other. However, if we find that the frequency a parent takes a small child to the library is strongly correlated to the children's interest in books we may be correct. If we are reasonably certain that the values in the X list cause the values in the Y list, we may safely interpolate within the range of values in the X list from the sample data to predict corresponding values in the Y list. However, it is much more dangerous to extrapolate. *Extrapolation* is making a prediction of a Y list value using an X list value outside the range the sample data. For example, if a positive correlation was found between hours of studying and lines of poetry memorized, the line of best fit would probably fail to be an appropriate model for additional lines of poetry memorized after several additional hours of study.

MODEL PROBLEM

Copy the data shown into L_1 and L_2 and make a scatter plot from the data. Looking at the scatter plot, describe the correlation, if any. Using the calculator, find the line of best fit. Find the value of r. Compare the correlation results to your estimate. Graph the line of best fit along with the scatter plot. Predict the L_2 value when L_1 is 210.

L_1	L_2
52	22
70	23
100	25
117	27
120	28
148	29
162	30
169	31
172	32
234	33
252	34
280	35

Solution:

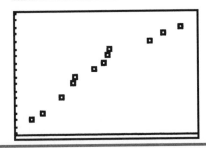

The points appear to have strong positive correlation. Use the calculator to find the line of best fit and the correlation coefficient.

The calculator will display:

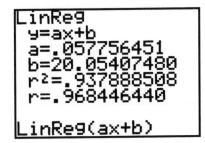

If you round your a and b values to the nearest hundredth and substitute them into the standard linear equation, the equation for the line of best fit is $y = 0.58x + 20.05$.

To graph the line of best fit indicate the lists and the Y subscript for the line.

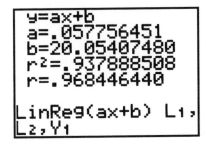

The graph will show that the scatter plot points are close to the line.

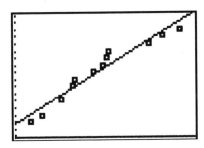

The value of r shown above, 0.968446440, verifies that there is a strong positive correlation between the two lists.

To find the value of L_2 when L_1 is 210, simply plug 210 into the equation of the line of best fit we found above; $y = 0.58x + 20.05$.

$y = 0.58(210) + 20.05$

$y = 141.85$

$y \approx 142$ **Answer**

Curve of Best Fit

There are many instances when the relationship between sets of data and the real world do not form linear patterns, therefore other possibilities are considered. A *curve of best fit* can be used to interpret data or make predictions about a set of data.

MODEL PROBLEM

If a cup of coffee is left on a countertop, it will cool off slowly. The scatter plot below shows the relationship between the temperature of a cup of coffee and how long it was left on a countertop.

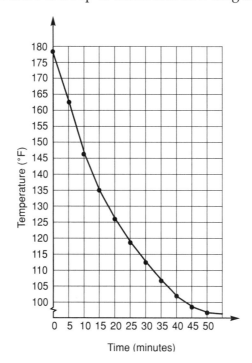

What is the temperature of a cup of coffee if it was left on a countertop for 20 minutes?

Solution:

You must find the temperature of the coffee when the cup has been left on the countertop for 20 minutes. The graph shows that the temperature of the coffee would be approximately 126 degrees.

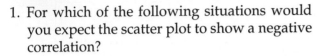
1. For which of the following situations would you expect the scatter plot to show a negative correlation?

   A The number of students in a high school and the average temperature of the city

   B The age of the car and the resale value

   C The price of an item and the amount of tax on the item

   D The speed of a car and the distance traveled in a fixed time

2. Which scatter plot shows a positive correlation?

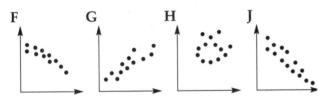

3. For which of the following situations would you expect the scatter plot to show no correlation?

   A Miles driven and gallons of gas used

   B Driving speed and driving time on a 5-mile stretch of highway

   C Number of pages in a book and number of copies sold

   D Oven temperature and cooking time for a 12-pound turkey

4. Which of the following could be the equation for the line of best fit for the scatter plot shown?

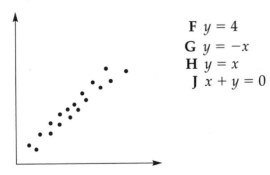

   F $y = 4$
   G $y = -x$
   H $y = x$
   J $x + y = 0$

5. The graph below shows how much Elyssa had saved each week for her digital camera. A curve of best fit has been drawn.

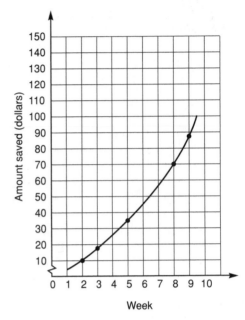

According to the curve of best fit, how much did Elyssa saved on the 6th week?

   A $48

   B $54

   C $60

   D $66

6. The graph below shows relationship between the length of a pendulum and the time required for the pendulum to complete one oscillation. A curve of best fit has been drawn.

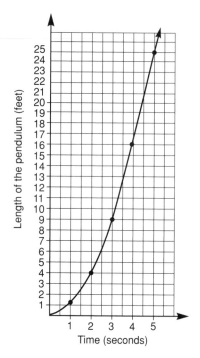

According to the curve of best fit, how long will it take a 2-foot-long pendulum to complete oscillation?

F 2.6 seconds

G 2 seconds

H 1.5 seconds

J 1 second

7. Display the data in a scatter plot and find the equation of the line of best fit.

x	10	10.5	11	12	9.5	13	10.5
y	47	35	63	22	55	27	9

8. Display the given data in a scatter plot and write an equation for the line of best fit.

x	21	35	42	56	60	65	70	75	85
y	12.5	19	23	30	34	34	37	39	44.5

9. The table shows the amount of study time students spend before a test and the test grade.

Study Time (in Hours)	Test Grade (in Percent)
10	90
5	80
4	72
12	94
3	68
6	87

Find the following.

- Create a scatter plot of the data.
- Draw a line of best fit and find its slope.
- Find the equation of the line of best fit.
- Using the equation for the line of best fit, predict the grade after 8 hours of study time.

10. Using the scatter plot, estimate what the value of new-home sales in the region might have been for 1995. Can you extrapolate a reasonable value for sales in 1997? Explain.

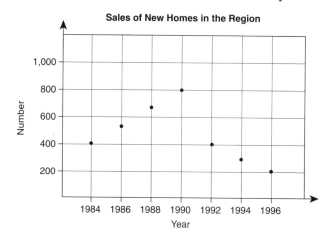

POPULATIONS AND SAMPLES

The entire group of objects or people involved in a statistical study is called a *population*. However, it is usually impossible to study a very large group. Hence a subset representative of the population, called a *sample*, is usually used in the study. The process of choosing the sample is called *sampling*. It is important to make sure the sample collected is unbiased and representative of the entire population. A *simple random sample* will give everyone or everything the same chance of being selected. A simple random sample does not involve more than one factor; for example, studying every tenth person who enters a shoe store. Simple random sampling is a valid method for gathering data such as customer gender and age.

MODEL PROBLEMS

1. The Cake Box surveyed people about the type of frosting they preferred on cakes. Use the results to predict how many of the 952 students at Washington High School would choose whipped cream.

Type of Frosting	Percent
whipped cream	55%
butter cream	40%
no preference	5%

Solution: Since 55% of the sample preferred whipped cream, finding 55% of 952 students allows you to make the prediction.

Answer: 0.55(952) = 523.6 or approximately 524 students

2. A quality tester finds three faulty batteries in a sample of 60 batteries. If there is a 2% margin of error, estimate the interval that contains the number of faulty batteries in a group of 3,000.

Solution: Let x = the number of faulty batteries in the group.

$$\frac{\text{faulty in sample}}{\text{total in sample}} = \frac{3}{60} = \frac{x}{3,000} = \frac{\text{faulty in group}}{\text{total in group}}$$

$$3(3,000) = 60x$$
$$9,000 = 60x$$
$$150 = x$$

Use the margin of error to estimate:

$$2\% \text{ of } 3,000 = (0.02)(3,000) = 60$$
$$\text{interval is } 150 - 60 \text{ to } 150 + 60$$

Answer: The interval is 90 to 210 batteries in the total group are faulty.

1. A sporting goods company surveyed 800 baseball players to see what type of bat they preferred. Aluminum bats were preferred over wood by 300 players. Which statement is true?

   A More than $\frac{1}{2}$ of the players surveyed preferred aluminum.

   B More than 40% of the players surveyed preferred aluminum.

   C More than 75% of the players surveyed did not prefer aluminum.

   D More than $\frac{1}{3}$ of the players surveyed preferred aluminum.

2. Which of the following samples is an example of an unbiased survey?

   F A simple random sample of 500 teens in the Northeast to determine the favorite music group for teens aged 13–15

   G A simple random sample of 500 men over 50 years of age to determine which brand of vitamins men over 50 prefer

   H A simple random sample of 250 women aged 18–35 to determine the favorite brand of ice cream of people 18–35

   J A simple random sample of 150 zoo visitors to determine if taxpayers feel that federal money should be used to help run the zoo

3. An office supply store surveyed a group of 200 students to determine their preference for backpack colors. Backpacks come in green, black, blue, and red. Based on the survey results the store will determine the color distribution for its order of 1,000 backpacks. If 75 chose black, 25 chose red, 40 chose green, and the rest chose blue, how many green backpacks will they order?

4. A television rating service found that 945 households out of a sample of 3,340 households watched the Super Bowl. Estimate to the nearest million how many of the 94 million households with a television watched the Super Bowl.

5. Biologists captured 400 deer, tagged them, and released them back into the same region. Later that season, the deer population was sampled to estimate the size of the population that lived in the region. If a sample of 150 deer contained 45 tagged deer, what would be a good estimate for the deer population in the region?

6. A quality tester finds two broken bulbs in every lot of 100. Suppose the margin of error is 3%. Estimate the interval that contains the number of broken bulbs in a lot of 5,000.

STATISTICAL MEASURES

A set of data, or values, can be described by using the *mean, median, mode*, or *range*. The mean, the median, and the mode are called *measures of central tendency*.

- The *mean* is the arithmetic *average*. It is found by dividing the sum of the values by the number of values.
- The *median* is the middle value when the values are listed in order. (*Note:* If the set contains an even number of values, the median is the average of the two values in the middle.)
- The *mode* is the value occurring most frequently.
- The *range* is the difference between the largest value and the smallest value.

To find the range, it is often helpful to arrange the members of the set from least to greatest (or vice versa). For example, when 84, 60, 89, 95, 63, and 74 are arranged in order, the range is obvious:

60, 63, 74, 84, 89, 95

Range = 95 − 60 = 35

The concept of range is important in quartiles and box-and-whisker plots.

The median of a data set divides the set into two equal parts, that is, two parts with the same number of members. *Quartiles* are values that separate a data set into four parts, each containing one-fourth or 25% of the members. For example:

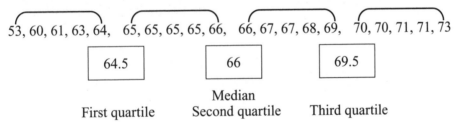

53, 60, 61, 63, 64,   65, 65, 65, 65, 66,   66, 67, 67, 68, 69,   70, 70, 71, 71, 73

| 64.5 | 66 | 69.5 |

Median

First quartile   Second quartile   Third quartile

- The *first* or *lower quartile* is the center of the lower half.
- The *second quartile* is the median.
- The *third* or *upper quartile* is the center of the upper half.
- The *interquartile range* is the difference between the third quartile and the first quartile. In the example of above, interquartile range = 69.5 − 64.5 = 5.

1. Debbie has the following scores on five math tests:

$$88 \quad 84 \quad 80 \quad 90 \quad 84$$

What score must she get on the sixth test in order for her average to fall between 85 and 87?

Solution: The sum of the six scores must be 6 times the average:

$$6 \times 85 = 510$$
$$6 \times 87 = 522$$

The sum of the first five scores is 426.

Answer: The sixth score must fall between 84 [510 − 426] and 96 [522 − 426].

2. Give a set of five scores such that the data would have

- a median of 60
- a mode of 52
- a mean of 65

Solution:

- $\underline{} \; \underline{} \; \underline{60} \; \underline{} \; \underline{}$
  If the median for five scores is 60, the third score must be 60. **Answer**

- $\underline{52} \; \underline{52} \; \underline{60} \; \underline{} \; \underline{}$
  Since the mode is 52, the lowest two scores must each be 52. **Answer**

- Since the mean is 65, the sum of the five scores must be $5 \times 65 = 325$. With 164 as the sum of the first three scores, the highest two scores must total $325 - 164$ or 161. Hence, the remaining two scores must be any two distinct numbers above 60 that total 161. For example, one solution is: 52, 52, 60, 80, 81. The solution is not unique. **Answer**

3. Find the quartiles and the interquartile range:

42, 25, 55, 58, 60, 75, 80, 85, 55, 19, 72, 77, 50

Solution:

Step 1 Arrange the members in ascending order:

19, 25, 42, 50, 55, 55, 58, 60, 65, 72, 75, 77, 80, 85

Step 2 Find the median. This is the second quartile:

19, 25, 42, 50, 55, 55, <u>58, 60</u>, 65, 72, 75, 77, 80, 85

Median = (58 + 60) ÷ 2 = 59

Step 3 First quartile is 50, the median of the seven values to the left of 59:

19, 25, 42, <u>50</u>, 55, 55, 58

Step 4 Third quartile is 75, the median of the seven values to the right of 59:

60, 65, 72, <u>75</u>, 77, 80, 85

Step 5 To find the interquartile range, subtract the first quartile from the third:

75 − 50 = 25

Answer: The quartiles are 50, 59, and 75. The interquartile range is 25.

Box-and-Whisker Plots

A *box-and-whisker* plot is a graph that describes data using the quartiles and the highest and lowest values (the *extreme* values) in the data. This plot is useful for comparing two or more data sets. The box-and-whisker plots show how the data for each are distributed and what the extreme values are.

To Construct a Box-and-Whisker Plot

- Draw a number line to include the lowest value and the highest value in the data set.
- Above the number line, mark the quartiles and the extreme values.
- Draw a box above the number line, with vertical sides passing through the lower and upper quartiles. Draw a vertical line in the box through the median (second quartile).
- Draw the "whiskers," horizontal lines extending from the vertical sides of the rectangle to the extreme values.

Note: **Outliers** are values much lower or much higher than most of the data. In a box-and-whisker plot, outliers are data that fall more than 1.5 times the interquartile range from quartiles. Do *not* extend whisker to any outliers.

MODEL PROBLEM

Construct a box-and-whisker plot for these data:
20 27 28 29 30 31 33 33 37 39 55

Solution:

Draw the box: The median is 31. The lower quartile is 28. The upper quartile is 37. Plot those values above a number line and draw the rectangle:

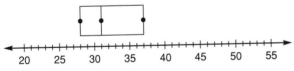

Draw the whiskers: The interquartile range is 37 − 28 = 9. Data more than 1.5(9) = 13.5 from the quartiles are outliers.

Left whisker:

28 − 13.5 = 14.5

No data are smaller than 14.5, so there are no low outliers. The left whisker will extend from the box to 20.

Right whisker:

37 + 13.5 = 50.5

One value, 55, is more than 50.5. The right whisker will therefore extend only to the next highest value, 39.

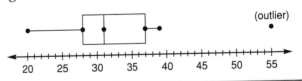

1. During a baseball season, the National League home-run champion had the following home-run statistics by month:

April	May	June	July	August	September	October
5	13	7	11	6	8	6

   Which month contains the median for the player's home-run statistics?

   A June   **C** August
   B July   **D** September

2. For each number shown in the box, the units digit is hidden. Which of the following could NOT be the mean of the set?

   $$8\triangle \quad 8\triangle \quad 7\triangle \quad 9\triangle \quad 8\triangle$$

   F 85   **G** 82   **H** 80   **J** 71

3. The following data represent morning temperatures for the month of July in Washington, D.C. What are the mean and median of the data?

   89 87 85 88 93 93 93 89 90 91 90 89 88 89 87 90
   91 92 92 92 90 89 87 85 86 84 84 83 85 86 88

   A Mean 84.3, median 91
   B Mean 82.9, median 90
   C Mean 88.5, median 89
   D Mean 83.9, median 88

4. For the given scores, the mean is 40:

   Scores: 20, 30, 40, 50, 60

   If the 20 is changed to a 17, which of the following would have to be done in order for the mean to remain at 40?

   F Change the 50 to a 47.
   G Change the 60 to a 57.
   H Change the 50 to a 53.
   J Change the 30 to a 27.

5. For a set of 6 scores, the following can be noted:

   > Score #1 is 6 points below the mean.
   >
   > Score #2 is 10 points below the mean.
   >
   > Score #3 is 4 points below the mean.
   >
   > Score #4 is equal to the mean.

   Which of the following could be TRUE about the remaining two scores?

   A Scores #5 and #6 are both equal to the mean.
   B Score #5 is 12 points above the mean and Score #6 is 8 points above the mean.
   C Score #5 is 10 points above the mean and Score #6 is 10 points below the mean.
   D Score #5 is 20 points above the mean and Score #6 is 4 points above the mean.

6. Which of the following statements will always be TRUE?

   I. The mode is always close to the median.
   II. The median is sometimes not included in the data.
   III. The mean is always included in the data.

   F I only
   G II only
   H III only
   J I and II only

7. Identify the first quartile:

   32, 24, 38, 26, 38, 36, 37, 39, 23, 40, 21, 31

   A 21   **B** 25   **C** 32   **D** 34

8. The interquartile range of a data set is 18. The first quartile is 52. What value could be the median?

   F 25   **G** 34   **H** 61   **J** 97

9. These box-and-whisker plots show test scores for two classes:

   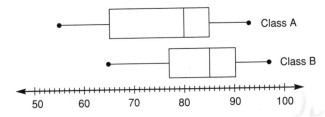

   Which statement is false?

   A The interquartile range is greater for class A than for class B.
   B The second quartile is higher for class B than for class A.
   C The lowest score was in class A.
   D Class A did better than class B.

10. The list shows the prices for several different concerts:

    $40 $45 $50 $58 $60 $67 $80 $90

    If an additional concert price of $16 is added to the list, which measure of central tendency is affected most?

11. Edgardo had the following test scores in his science class:

    90 73 86 89 97

    What score must he get on the sixth test in order for his average to turn out to be 89?

12. The mean for a set of 5 scores is 60. The mean for a different set of 10 scores is 90. What is the mean for all 15 scores?

13. Give three different values for x so that 80 would be the median.

Score	Number of Students
90	4
85	2
80	3
75	x
70	4

14. Mr. Abbott asked his math students to use the following data to find average test scores.

Mr. Abbott's Classes

Period	No. of Students	Test Average
1 Algebra	20	80
2 Algebra	20	70
3 Geometry	30	84
5 Geometry	10	80

In computing the average test score for the combined algebra classes, Bill suggested that Mr. Abbott take the average of 80 and 70 to get 75. For the two combined geometry classes, however, using the same approach gives a wrong result of 82. Explain why the first average (75) was correct but the second average (82) was NOT correct. Find the correct average for the two geometry classes. Explain your approach.

15. A class decided to compare a supermarket brand chocolate chip cookie with a famous name brand. The students broke apart nine cookies of each brand and recorded the number of chips. Construct a box-and-whisker plot for each brand and compare the data, including quartiles, interquartiles, and the length of the whiskers.

Supermarket Brand	Name Brand
4	7
4	7
5	8
5	9
6	9
7	9
10	10
12	10
18	11

3.6 DATA DISPLAYS

Data can be organized and displayed by using a variety of different graphs. Tables and charts are also commonly used to display data. The type of graph or device used is determined by the nature of the data and what the data are intended to communicate.

A *stem-and-leaf plot* is a display that shows each data value.

MODEL PROBLEM

In September, each of the 24 students in a math class reported the number of days he or she worked that summer:

25, 17, 15, 28, 24, 13, 16, 28, 19, 25, 24, 36, 33, 18, 24, 38, 28, 25, 27, 14, 37, 28, 35, 43

Represent these data in a stem-and-leaf plot, with the values in the *tens* place as the stem and the corresponding values in the *units* place as the leaves.

Solution:

Step 1 Find the smallest and largest values in the data.
Step 2 Draw a vertical line. To the left of the line, write each consecutive digit from the smallest stem value to the largest stem value.
Step 3 Insert the leaves.
Step 4 For each stem, reorder the leaves from the smallest to largest.
Step 5 Include a key

For the data above, the smallest value is 13 and the largest value is 43. The smallest tens value is 1 and the largest tens value is 4. After step 3, the plot looks like this:

```
1 | 7 5 3 6 9 8 4
2 | 5 8 4 8 5 4 4 8 5 7 8
3 | 6 3 8 7 5
4 | 3
```

After Step 4; ordering the leaves, the plot looks like this:

```
1 | 3 4 5 6 7 8 9
2 | 4 4 4 5 5 5 7 8 8 8 8
3 | 3 5 6 7 8
4 | 3
```

The key (Step 5) can show any value, such as 2 | 4 = 24.
From this plot, we find that most students worked from 24 to 28 days.

A *circle graph* is used to compare parts of a whole. It is sometimes called a *pie chart*.

Profits From Local Carnival

A *bar graph* compares amounts of quantities.

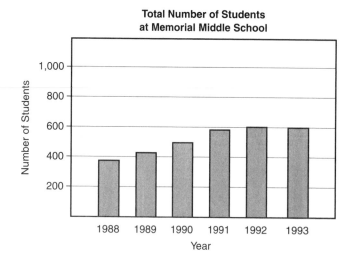

A *pictograph* also compares amounts. A symbol is used to represent a stated amount.

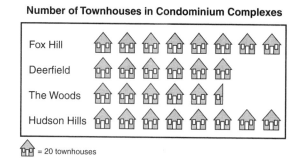

A *histogram* is a bar graph used to show frequencies. In a histogram, the bars, which usually represent grouped intervals, are adjacent.

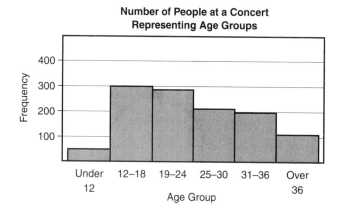

A *line graph* shows continuous change and trends over time.

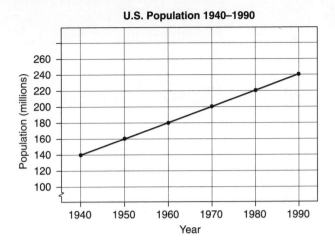

A *line plot* is another way to organize frequency data. A line plot is a picture of the data on a number line corresponding to the range of the data.

As is shown in the example above, in a line plot you place an x (or a dot) above the appropriate number to indicate each occurrence.

MODEL PROBLEM

You need to construct a graph showing the trend in the price of a gallon of gasoline each month over a five-year period of time. Which of the following types of displays would be most appropriate?

A Circle graph
B Histogram
C Line plot
D Line graph

Solution: Since the situation depicts changing prices over a period of time, the most appropriate display would be the line graph.

A circle graph is not appropriate since you are not looking at parts of a whole.

A histogram is not appropriate since you are not comparing intervals of prices.

A line plot is not appropriate since you are not organizing frequency data.

1. Which of the following types of graphs would NOT be an appropriate representation to depict the way a family budgets its September income?

   A Bar graph   **C** Circle graph

   B Pictograph   **D** Line graph

2. Using the given pictograph, what percent of the total number of cars sold at Thrifty's in September did Dan sell?

   F 60%   **G** 40%   **H** 30%   **J** 20%

   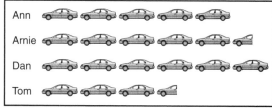

   Number of Cars Sold at Thrifty's in September

   = 10 cars

3. Use the given circle graph to determine what percent of Tim's exercise program is devoted to running.

   A 25%

   B 40%

   C 60%

   D $66\frac{2}{3}\%$

   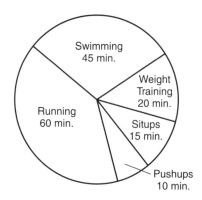

4. For which of the following situations would it NOT be appropriate to use a line graph to represent the data?

   F Show the population of the U.S. from 1900 to 1990

   G Show the sale of CD's during a five-year period

   H Show survey results of how students spend one hour of their time

   J Show the heating time for water at various altitudes

5. The key for a stem-and-leaf plot is $4\,|\,7 = 47$. The value 63 would be plotted as:

   A $3\,|\,6$ **B** $60\,|\,3$ **C** $6\,|\,3$ **D** 63

6. The weights of pumpkins sold at a farmer's market are given below. Construct a stem-and-leaf plot for the weights.

   Pumpkin Weights (lb)

19	11	10	8	12	15
7	22	17	23	25	17

7. Assuming that this circle graph applies to the city of Metropolis, which has 42,000 homes, how many homes are NOT heated by natural gas?

   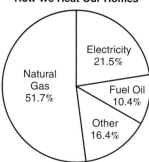

8. The South Side High School annual fund-raiser involved the sale of tins of cookies. The freshmen class sold 2,586 tins of cookies; the sophomore class 3,014 tins; the junior class 3,274 tins; and the senior class 3,326 tins.

Construct a graph to show how the classes compared in amounts of cookies sold. Explain why you selected that type of graph to represent the data.

9. Test scores in a biology class are as follows: 83, 78, 94, 93, 87, 86, 83, 94, 99, 90, 87, 79, 65, 87, 93, 96, 88, 84, 82, 93, 85.

   • Construct a line plot for the data.
   • State the median score for the data.

10. This graph shows the percentages of pickle buyers who selected various types of pickles.

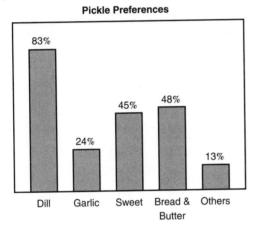

Pickle Preferences

   • Explain why the data cannot be used to construct a circle graph.
   • Explain what is wrong or misleading in the given graph.

11. The line plot displays scores on an 80-point mathematics test.

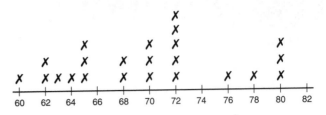

   • Which measure of central tendency (mean, median, or mode) is most easily observed from this line plot? Explain why.
   • What is the median test score? Explain how you find it from this line plot.
   • Suppose the teacher finds six scores that need to be added to the line plot: 72, 76, 76, 78, 80, 80.
      (i) Does the median change? If so, what is the new median?
      (ii) Does the mode change? If so, what is the new mode?
      (iii) In a general way, how does the mean change and why? (Do not actually calculate the mean.)

12. Aggie, a camp counselor, recorded the high temperature at camp each day. Construct a stem-and-leaf plot for the temperatures (°F) in July.

78, 79, 80, 86, 82, 90, 91, 91, 89, 94, 89, 95, 94, 91, 88, 86, 91, 87, 90, 88, 92, 90, 94, 93

A *matrix* (plural: *matrices*) is a rectangular arrangement of numbers corresponding to the real-world situation involving data. In a matrix the numbers are arranged in rows and columns. The number of rows (horizontal) and the number of columns (vertical) determine the dimension of the matrix. The 3-by-2 matrix below displays the sales of a particular new car by three dealers in June vs. July.

$$\begin{array}{c} \\ \text{Dealer 1} \\ \text{Dealer 2} \\ \text{Dealer 3} \end{array} \begin{array}{cc} \text{June} & \text{July} \\ \left[\begin{array}{cc} 20 & 12 \\ 3 & 11 \\ 10 & 7 \end{array}\right] \end{array}$$

MODEL PROBLEM

Write a matrix showing the mileage and gas expenses used by S. Teasley, R. Brown, and T. Cox for the month of September.

September Monthly Travel Expenses

Name	Mileage	Gas Cost
S. Teasley	400	$32.00
R. Brown	220	$17.60
T. Cox	530	$42.40

Solution:

$$\begin{array}{c} \\ \text{S. Teasley} \\ \text{R. Brown} \\ \text{T. Cox} \end{array} \begin{array}{cc} \text{Mileage} & \text{Gas Cost} \\ \left[\begin{array}{cc} 400 & 32 \\ 220 & 17.6 \\ 530 & 42.4 \end{array}\right] \end{array}$$

Matrix Addition, Subtraction, and Scalar Multiplication

Scalar Multiplication is the operation of multiplying a matrix by a real number, k. The answer, a new matrix, is the result of multiplying each element in the given matrix by k. For example:

If $A = \begin{bmatrix} 0 & 1 \\ 2 & 5 \end{bmatrix}$, find 2A.

Solution:

$$2\begin{bmatrix} 0 & 1 \\ 2 & 5 \end{bmatrix} = \begin{bmatrix} 2 \cdot 0 & 2 \cdot 1 \\ 2 \cdot 2 & 2 \cdot 5 \end{bmatrix} = \begin{bmatrix} 0 & 2 \\ 4 & 10 \end{bmatrix}$$

Two matrices can be added to or subtracted from each other if they have the same dimensions. The result will be a new matrix that represents the addition or subtraction of the two matrices. The following are two rules to remember when adding and subtracting matrices.

- When *adding* two matrices, remember to find the sum of the corresponding elements of the matrices.
- When *subtracting* two matrices, remember to find the differences of the corresponding elements of the matrices.

MODEL PROBLEMS

1. Let $A = \begin{bmatrix} 1 & 2 \\ 3 & 5 \end{bmatrix}$ and $B = \begin{bmatrix} 6 & {}^-8 \\ {}^-4 & 7 \end{bmatrix}$. Find $A + 2B$.

Solution:

$$A + 2B = \begin{bmatrix} 1 + (6 \cdot 2) & 2 + ({}^-8 \cdot 2) \\ 3 + ({}^-4 \cdot 2) & 5 + (7 \cdot 2) \end{bmatrix} = \begin{bmatrix} 1 + 12 & 2 + ({}^-16) \\ 3 + ({}^-8) & 5 + 14 \end{bmatrix} = \begin{bmatrix} 13 & {}^-14 \\ {}^-5 & 19 \end{bmatrix}$$

2. Let $D = \begin{bmatrix} {}^-6 & 4 \\ 2 & {}^-3 \end{bmatrix}$ and $E = \begin{bmatrix} 8 & {}^-2 \\ 0 & {}^-1 \end{bmatrix}$. Find $D - E$.

Solution:

$$D - E = \begin{bmatrix} {}^-6 - 8 & 4 - ({}^-2) \\ 2 - 0 & {}^-3 - ({}^-1) \end{bmatrix} = \begin{bmatrix} {}^-14 & 6 \\ 2 & {}^-2 \end{bmatrix}$$

3. Two companies make three different toys for three different ages: baby (B), toddler (T), and Child (C). The matrices below show the number of toys, in thousands, each company makes in one day.

Company 1

	B	T	C
Toy 1	2	6	0
Toy 2	7	18	15
Toy 3	4	25	9

Company 2

	B	T	C
Toy 1	1	9	4
Toy 2	8	3	7
Toy 3	3	0	15

How many of the toddler products are made by both companies?

Solution:

The amount of toddler products produced by Company 1 can be represented by the following matrix:

$$\begin{array}{c} \\ \text{Toy 1} \\ \text{Toy 2} \\ \text{Toy 3} \end{array} \begin{array}{c} T \\ \begin{bmatrix} 6 \\ 18 \\ 25 \end{bmatrix} \end{array}$$

The amount of toddler products produced by Company 2 can be represented by the following matrix:

$$\begin{array}{c} \\ \text{Toy 1} \\ \text{Toy 2} \\ \text{Toy 3} \end{array} \begin{array}{c} T \\ \begin{bmatrix} 9 \\ 3 \\ 0 \end{bmatrix} \end{array}$$

Add both matrices to find how many of the toddler products are made by both companies.

$$\begin{array}{c} \text{Toy 1} \\ \text{Toy 2} \\ \text{Toy 3} \end{array} \begin{bmatrix} 6 + 9 \\ 18 + 3 \\ 25 + 0 \end{bmatrix} = \begin{bmatrix} 15 \\ 21 \\ 25 \end{bmatrix}$$

Use the table below for problems 1 and 2.

Attendance at the Football Game

Game	Freshmen	Sophomores	Juniors	Seniors	Other People
1	200	143	111	157	259
2	306	104	124	308	352
3	153	213	109	151	204
4	322	200	100	252	20

1. Which matrix represents the attendance at game 3?

   A $[200 \ 143 \ 111 \ 157 \ 259]$

   B $\begin{bmatrix} 157 \\ 308 \\ 151 \\ 252 \end{bmatrix}$

   C $[153 \ 213 \ 109 \ 151 \ 204]$

   D $[322 \ 200 \ 100 \ 252 \ 50]$

2. Which matrix represents the attendance at the games by juniors and seniors?

   F $\begin{bmatrix} 153 & 213 & 109 & 151 \\ 322 & 200 & 100 & 252 \end{bmatrix}$

   G $\begin{bmatrix} 111 & 157 \\ 124 & 308 \\ 109 & 151 \\ 100 & 252 \end{bmatrix}$

   H $\begin{bmatrix} 143 & 157 \\ 104 & 308 \\ 213 & 151 \\ 200 & 252 \end{bmatrix}$

   J $\begin{bmatrix} 200 & 157 \\ 306 & 308 \\ 153 & 151 \\ 322 & 252 \end{bmatrix}$

3. Given

   $A = \begin{bmatrix} 56 & 73 \\ 69 & 84 \end{bmatrix}$
   $B = \begin{bmatrix} 29 & 41 \\ 37 & 52 \end{bmatrix}$

   What is the value of 2A + B?

   A $\begin{bmatrix} 85 & 114 \\ 106 & 136 \end{bmatrix}$

   B $\begin{bmatrix} 114 & 155 \\ 143 & 188 \end{bmatrix}$

   C $\begin{bmatrix} 141 & 187 \\ 175 & 220 \end{bmatrix}$

   D $\begin{bmatrix} 170 & 228 \\ 212 & 272 \end{bmatrix}$

4. For $T = \begin{bmatrix} 2 & 8 \\ -7 & 5 \end{bmatrix}$ and $U = \begin{bmatrix} -1 & -5 \\ 6 & 4 \end{bmatrix}$, what is $T - U$?

   F $\begin{bmatrix} 3 & 13 \\ -13 & 1 \end{bmatrix}$

   G $\begin{bmatrix} 3 & 3 \\ -13 & 1 \end{bmatrix}$

   H $\begin{bmatrix} 1 & 3 \\ -1 & 1 \end{bmatrix}$

   J $\begin{bmatrix} 1 & 13 \\ -1 & 9 \end{bmatrix}$

5. The Green Thumb Club sold shirts in the styles and sizes shown in the matrix below. The Clean Air Club sold three times as much as the Green Thumb Club.

Green Thumb Club Shirts

	M	L	XL
Short Sleeve	15	35	40
Long Sleeve	10	8	25

What was the total number of medium shirts that were sold by the Clean Air Club?

A 25

B 45

C 30

D 75

6. Let $B = \begin{bmatrix} 17 & ^-30 \\ 0 & 40 \\ 2 & 8 \end{bmatrix}$ and $C = \begin{bmatrix} 5 & 0 \\ 2 & ^-1 \\ 2 & 13 \end{bmatrix}$.

Find $2C - B$.

7. What is the element in the first row and second column of the matrix that is result of $2A + B$ if $A = \begin{bmatrix} 2 & ^-3 \\ 4 & ^-6 \end{bmatrix}$ and $B = \begin{bmatrix} ^-6 & ^-11 \\ 3 & 9 \end{bmatrix}$?

8. The matrix below shows how much of each kind of food was sold on the first and second day of the fall carnival.

	1st day	2nd day
Candy Apples	144	305
Cotton Candy	215	114
Sodas	505	423
Chips	413	405

How much Cotton Candy was sold on the two days?

9. The matrices below represent the number of tickets of each type of seats sold for a performance musical play on Saturday and Wednesday.

Saturday

	Matinees	Evening
Orchestra	275	295
Mezzanine	143	158
Balcony	65	87

Wednesday

	Matinees	Evening
Orchestra	220	251
Mezzanine	133	140
Balcony	52	45

If orchestra seats cost $50, mezzanine seats $45, and balcony seats $30, how much more did the theatre make on the two evening performances compared to the two matinee performances?

10. The two matrices below represent the enrollment for grades nine to twelve at Lincoln High School and Central High School.

Lincoln H.S.

	9	10	11	12
Male	155	211	168	198
Female	173	194	165	181

Central H.S.

	9	10	11	12
Male	211	204	176	188
Female	179	209	167	193

Answer the following:
- How many 9th graders are there at Lincoln High School?
- How many male 11th graders are at the two high schools combined?
- How many more female 10th graders are there than female 12th graders at the two schools combined?
- Which school has the greater total enrollment?

To use a graph to interpret data:

- Pay attention to the scale. Check to see if the scale has a broken line between zero and the first interval.
- Know what the numbers mean.
- Read the title and the labels on the axes.
- Check graphs with multiple lines or bars for relationships between points.
- Be able to make predictions about the relation that *goes beyond* what is displayed. This is called ***extrapolation***.

To use a table to interpret data:

- Read the title and labels.
- Know what the numbers mean.
- Be able to estimate values *between* given entries. This is called ***interpolation***.

When interpreting data, be alert for misuses and abuses of statistics. Statistics can be misleading if:

- An inappropriate scale is used to display data.

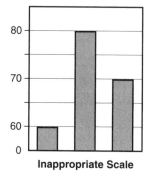

Inappropriate Scale

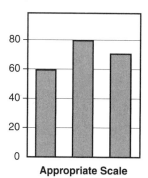

Appropriate Scale

- The wrong measure of central tendency is used to describe the data.
  In a small company of six people, the salaries of individuals are $80,000; $20,000; $25,000; $19,000; $22,500; $23,500. The average salary is about $32,000. Using the average would be inappropriate to describe the set. A better descriptor of the data would be the median, $23,000.
- Insufficient titles or labels are used on the axes or chart.

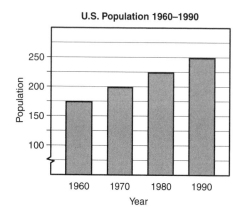

U.S. Population 1960–1990

The vertical axis doesn't indicate that the numbers are in millions.

- The graphic has a visual distortion to suggest a disproportionate relation, thus not accurately illustrating the numerical relationship.

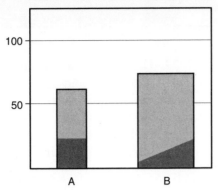

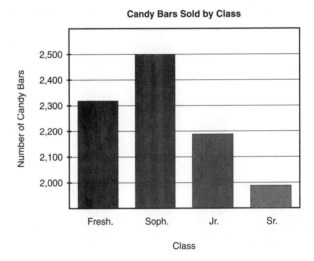

MODEL PROBLEMS

1. The graph displays the average monthly temperatures for two different years. How do the temperatures for Year A compare to those for Year B? Explain.

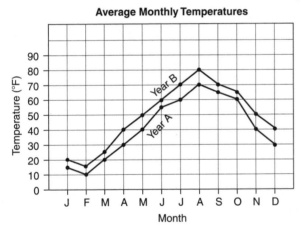

Average Monthly Temperatures

Solution: The graph of the average monthly temperatures for Year B is above the graph for Year A, indicating that the average monthly temperatures for Year B were greater than those for Year A. Since the two graphs never intersect, it is clear that at no time did a month in Year B record a temperature less than or equal to the same month for Year A.

2. What impression is given by the graph? How is this impression created?

Candy Bars Sold by Class

Solution: The graph suggests that the sophomore class sold significantly more candy bars than the senior class. The scale gives the same amount of space to the interval 0–2,000 as to the intervals of one hundred. This is inappropriate.

1. The following graph shows the average monthly 6:00 A.M. and 6:00 P.M. temperatures (°F) recorded at Newark Airport.

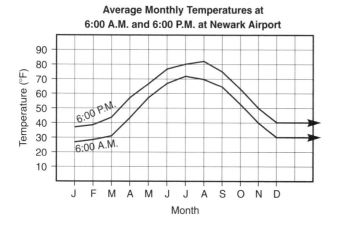

Average Monthly Temperatures at
6:00 A.M. and 6:00 P.M. at Newark Airport

Answer the following.
- How do you know that the graph does NOT show a situation in which the September temperatures at 6:00 A.M. and 6:00 P.M. were the same?

- According to the graph, was there any month when the average 6:00 A.M. temperature was greater than the average 6:00 P.M. temperature? Explain your response.

2. The circle graphs show how Sally and Michele spend their earnings. How is it possible that Michele can spend a greater dollar amount on recreation than the dollar amount spent by Sally?

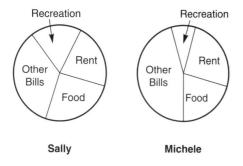

Sally   Michele

3. The graph shows the volume of sales of cassette tapes and compact discs (CD's) at a local music store over a six-year period. Explain the trend shown separately in Line A and Line B. Discuss the significance of the point of intersection of Line A and Line B.

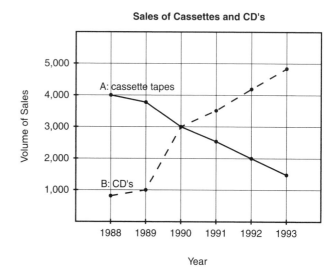

Sales of Cassettes and CD's

4. The graph is intended to compare morning coffee sales at two convenience stores in the same town. Is the visual message depicted in the graph accurate? Explain your response.

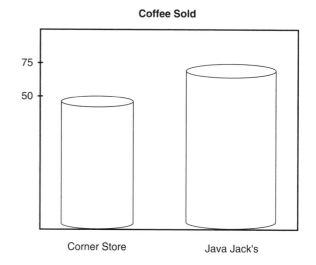

Coffee Sold

Corner Store   Java Jack's

5. Mrs. Mendez is giving a dinner party. She plans to serve a $5\frac{3}{4}$-pound standing rib roast that she plans to cook in a microwave oven. She knows that her guests prefer the meat to be cooked medium. Using the information shown, what is the minimum amount of time (in minutes) needed to cook the roast?

BEEF	Microwave Time		Internal Temperature	
	Step 1 HIGH (100%)	Step 2 MED-HIGH (70%)	At Removal	After Standing
Standing or Rolled Rib	Less than 4 lb: $6\frac{1}{2}$ min More than 4 lb: $10\frac{1}{2}$ min	Rare: 9–13 min/lb Medium: 10–$13\frac{1}{2}$ min/lb Well Done: $10\frac{1}{2}$–15 min/lb	120° 135° 150°	140° 150° 160°
Tenderloin	Less than 2 lb: 4 min More than 2 lb: $6\frac{1}{2}$ min	Rare: 8–11 min/lb Medium: 9–13 min/lb Well Done: $10\frac{1}{2}$–$14\frac{1}{2}$ min/lb	120° 135° 150°	140° 150° 160°

1. Two dice are rolled. What is the probability that either the sum is 3 or the sum is 8?

    A $\frac{7}{36}$ **B** $\frac{1}{6}$ **C** $\frac{5}{36}$ **D** $\frac{1}{12}$

2. Which of the following is TRUE about the data?

Score	Frequency
80	2
82	4
86	3
90	5

    F The mean is greater than the median.
    G The median is greater than the mean.
    H The mean equals the median.
    J There is no mode for the data.

3. Data that describes a situation in which any value between two given values can theoretically occur is called *continuous data*. Continuous data often results from measurements.

    If the data is not continuous, it is called *discrete*. Discrete data comes from counting situations.

    Which of the following situations illustrates discrete data?

    A Temperatures recorded every half hour at a weather station
    B Lengths of 1,000 bolts of fabric produced in a factory
    C The heights of individuals
    D The number of children in a family

4. This table shows the amounts of candy sold by the classes in Washington High School.

Candy Sale Results	
Freshmen	11,200
Sophomores	9,600
Juniors	11,700
Seniors	7,500

    Which graph is the POOREST representation of the data?

    F
    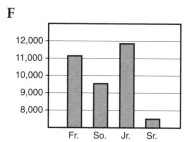

    G
    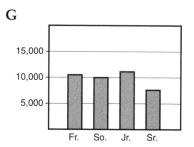

    H
    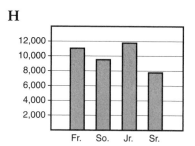

    J
    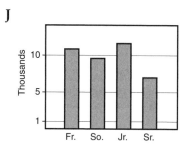

5. Which of the following situations represents events that are *independent*? (That is, the outcome of the first event has no effect on the outcome of the second event.)

   A Two marbles are selected from a container without replacement.

   B Two children born in a family are a boy, then a girl.

   C A ticket is selected for second prize after the first-prize ticket has been removed.

   D A king is selected from a deck of cards after two kings have already been dealt.

6. A theater did a survey of the ages of people who came to their cabaret. The table summarizes the results. Find the median age of the viewers.

   F 13–30
   G 31–48
   H 49–66
   J over 66

Ages	Numbers
12 and under	87
13–30	298
31–48	481
49–66	364
over 66	95

7. The rules for a board game call for a player to lose a turn if the player rolls three consecutive doubles on a pair of dice. What is the probability that a player will lose a turn in her first three rolls?

   A $\frac{1}{6}$ B $\frac{1}{18}$ C $\frac{1}{36}$ D $\frac{1}{216}$

8. A basketball player with a free throw shooting average of 60% is on the line for a one-and-one free throw (the player gets a second shot if the first shot is successful). What is the probability the player will score two points at the free-throw line?

   F 0.6   G 0.4   H 0.36   J 0.24

9. If y varies directly with x then when x is doubled y will ___.

   A not change   C increase by 2
   B be halved   D be doubled

10. Given the set of data: 92, 80, 79, 75, 75, 58, 55. If the 58 and 55 were dropped from the data, which measure would remain unchanged?

    F Median
    G Mode
    H Mean
    J Range

11. The histogram shows final averages of the students enrolled in Algebra at the North End High School.

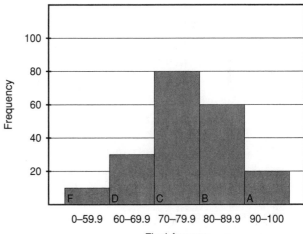

What percent of the students scored B or better in the course?

    A 20%
    B 40%
    C 60%
    D 80%

12. For which of the following situations would you use the entire population rather than a sample?

   F A cook making sauce wants to know if there is enough salt in it.
   G The president of the company wants to know how many people are going to the company Holiday Party.
   H A statistical research company wants to know how many households watched the Academy Awards show.
   J A medical research group wants to study the blood cholesterol levels of women in the United States over age 50.

13. For which of the following situations would you use the mean to analyze the data?

   A The preferred color marker students buy
   B The day of the week on which most students were born
   C The grades in class received on a test
   D The difference between the age of the oldest and youngest students in the class

14. If a pair of dice is rolled, what is the probability of getting a sum of 8?

15. The mean of a set of 10 scores is 61. What is the sum of the 10 scores?

16. Eight scores have a mean of 30. The bottom two scores have a mean of 21. The top two scores have a mean of 50. What is the mean of the four middle scores?

17. There are 20 students in a class. The average grade for the class on a test was computed as 74, but one student's grade was read mistakenly as 50 instead of 90. What will the average grade for that class be when it is recomputed using the correct score?

18. A simple random sample of 50 fish in a lake were captured and tagged. Two weeks later, a random sample of 27 fish contains 3 with tags. Estimate the number of fish in the lake.

19. The chart below indicates the costs at a local copy center. Martina, a member of the center, needs to have 75 copies made of a packet containing 22 pages. She needs the packets collated and stapled. Furthermore, she wants the copies run on three-hole-punch paper. What will be the cost of the job?

Copying

# SETS PER ORIGINAL	PRICE PER COPY	
	MEMBER	NONMEMBER
1	0.05	0.06
2–49	0.04	0.05
50–499	0.03	0.04
500–900	0.025	0.035
1,000+	0.02	0.03
ADDITIONAL SERVICES (add to copy charges)		
Collating		Free
Stapling		0.02/Staple
Hand Feeding		0.10/Page
Reducing		0.25/Setting
OTHER STOCK (add to copy charges)		
Legal Size Paper		0.01/Page
3-Hole-Punch Paper		0.01/Page
Pastel #20 Paper		0.01/Page
Bright #60 Paper		0.02/Page
Résumé Stock		0.05/Page
Card Stock		0.05/Page
Mailing Labels		0.30/Page
Transparencies		0.40/Page
Minimum order $1.00		

20. The matrices show the high and low temperatures in degrees Fahrenheit for selected towns for the months of June and December. The columns represent the high and low temperatures. The rows show the cities.

$$
\begin{array}{cc}
 & \text{June} \\
 & \begin{array}{cc} \text{high} & \text{low} \end{array} \\
\begin{array}{l} \text{Baltimore} \\ \text{Cumberland} \\ \text{Aberdeen} \end{array} &
\begin{bmatrix} 70 & 56 \\ 95 & 75 \\ 87 & 54 \end{bmatrix}
\end{array}
\qquad
\begin{array}{cc}
 & \text{December} \\
 & \begin{array}{cc} \text{high} & \text{low} \end{array} \\
 &
\begin{bmatrix} 28 & 5 \\ 40 & 18 \\ 35 & 22 \end{bmatrix}
\end{array}
$$

Create a matrix that indicates the changes in the high and low temperatures for the three towns from June to December.

21. The following data represent the heights in inches of students in a kindergarten class. Construct a line plot from the data. State the median, the mode, and the mean for the data.

    48 47 44 46 48 46 42 46 51

    46 50 43 42 45 43 47 49

22. Construct a bar graph from the information in this table.

Nicole's Fall Fund-Raiser Sales	
Gift Bags	ℕℕℕℕℕℕ |||
Rolls of Wrap	ℕℕℕ |||
Bags of Bows	ℕℕ |||
Gift Tabs	ℕℕ	

23. A discount clothing store has the following policy. Each week that an item remains on the rack it is discounted by 10% of its current price.

    • A suit is originally priced at $450. Generate a table to show the price of the suit for the first six weeks it is on the rack.
    • Write a formula to generalize the sequence produced in the previous part.
    • Determine the number of weeks it will take for the suit to be priced less than $100.

24. Two dice are rolled.

    • Explain why the probability of obtaining a sum less than or equal to 5 is the same as the probability of obtaining a sum greater than or equal to 9.
    • If the probability of obtaining a sum less than or equal to 6 is the same as the probability of obtaining a sum greater than or equal to k, find the value of k.
    • If three dice are rolled, what is the probability that the sum obtained is less than or equal to 3?
    • The answer above would be the same as the probability that the sum obtained is greater than or equal to what value?

25. A school offers baseball, soccer, and basketball to its 120 students. A survey showed that 35 students played baseball, 70 played soccer, 40 played basketball, 20 played both soccer and basketball, 15 played both soccer and baseball, 15 played both basketball and baseball, and 10 played all three sports.

    • How many students played none of the three sports?
    • What percent of the students played baseball as their only sport?
    • How many students played both basketball and baseball, but not soccer?

26. Construct a scatter plot using the following information. Draw the line of best fit and find the equation.

Time Spent Doing Homework vs. Viewing Television		
Student	Homework (min)	Television Viewing (min)
A	30	60
B	90	45
C	90	0
D	75	90
E	60	120
F	75	30
G	45	60
H	60	0
I	0	180
J	45	30

27. Use the data in the table to answer the following.

U.S. Population	
Year	Population (millions)
1890	63
1900	76
1910	92
1920	106
1930	123
1940	132
1950	151
1960	179
1970	203
1980	227
1990	249
2000	281

- Draw a line graph of the data given in the table.
- *Interpolation* is the process of estimating a value between two known values. Using the graph, interpolate to find the U.S. population in 1975.
- Examine the population changes between 1980–1990 and 1990–2000. Predict what the population might be in the year 2010 if this pattern continues. Explain your reasoning.

28. The table lists the life expectancies in years of males as estimated in 2003.

Age in Years	Expected Years Until Death
0	75.4
10	66.0
20	56.3
30	47.0
40	37.6
50	28.8
60	20.6
70	13.5

Find the following:

- Create a scatter plot of the data.
- Find the equation of the line of best fit.
- Using the equation of the line of best fit predict the life expectancy of males at age 80.

Cumulative Assessment

For Chapters 1, 2, and 3

1. How many three-digit numbers have all of the following characteristics?

    I. The number is a multiple of 72.
    II. The number is divisible by 5.
    III. The number is less than 500.

    A 0   **B** 1   **C** 2   **D** 5

2. Which of the following is NOT equal to the other numbers?

    F 0.2   **G** $\sqrt{\dfrac{1}{25}}$ **H** $\dfrac{1}{2} + \dfrac{1}{3}$ **J** $\dfrac{0.05}{0.25}$

3. A school club consists of only juniors and seniors. If the ratio of juniors to seniors in the club is $3:2$, which of the following could NOT be the total number of club members?

    A 16   **B** 20   **C** 25   **D** 30

4. Using four of the five digits 1, 3, 4, 7, 8, how many four-digit numbers can be formed, with no repetition of digits, if the number must be odd?

    F 625   **G** 120   **H** 72   **J** 36

5. Three dice are rolled. What is the probability of obtaining a sum that is less than or equal to 4?

    A $\dfrac{1}{216}$ **B** $\dfrac{1}{108}$ **C** $\dfrac{1}{72}$ **D** $\dfrac{1}{54}$

6. This list shows test scores for fifteen students:

    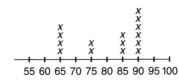

    Which of the following is true about the data?

    F The mean equals the median.
    G The median is greater than the mean.
    H The median is less than the mean.
    J There is no mode for the data.

7. During a recent month, the exchange rate of Canadian dollars to United States dollars was 1 to 0.81. If you paid $65 in Canadian dollars for a toaster-oven, what would you have paid in United States dollars? (Disregard tax.)

    A $52.65
    B $65.81
    C $80.25
    D $84.00

8. About what percent of the big square is shaded?

    F 5%
    G 15%
    H 20%
    J 25%

9. Daniel, David, and Darryl independently answer a question on a test. The probability that Daniel answers correctly is .9. The probability that David answers correctly is .6. The probability that Darryl answers correctly is .8. What is the probability that not one of the three answers the question correctly?

    A .008   **B** .432   **C** .568   **D** .72

10. There are four times as many boys as girls on the newspaper staff of Central High School. If there are 40 staff members in all, how many of them are girls?

    F 8   **G** 10   **H** 30   **J** 32

11. Lin bought a sweater at 30% off the original price. The discount saved him $12.60. What was the original price of the sweater?

    A $8.82   **C** $29.40
    B $21.42   **D** $42.00

12. The population in Culver Heights increased from 1990 to 1993 as shown in the table. What was the average annual percent increase in population over the three-year period?

Years	Population
1990 to 1991	10,000 to 11,000
1991 to 1992	11,000 to 12,000
1992 to 1993	12,000 to 13,000

F 8.33%

G 9.14%

H 10%

J 27.42%

13. Set G consists of the three-digit multiples of 3. Set H consists of the three-digit multiples of 4. Set L consists of the three-digit multiples of 6.

Which of the following statements is true about the three sets of numbers?

A If a number is in Set G, it is also in Set L.

B The smallest number contained in all three sets is 144.

C If a number is in Set L, it is also in Set G.

D No multiple of 9 is in Set H.

14. Which of the following represents the sum of the matrices $\begin{bmatrix} 2 & 20 \\ 40 & ^-10 \end{bmatrix}$ and $\begin{bmatrix} 3 & ^-10 \\ 24 & 8 \end{bmatrix}$?

F $\begin{bmatrix} ^-1 & ^-30 \\ 16 & ^-2 \end{bmatrix}$

G $\begin{bmatrix} 5 & ^-30 \\ 64 & ^-18 \end{bmatrix}$

H $\begin{bmatrix} 5 & 10 \\ 64 & ^-2 \end{bmatrix}$

J $\begin{bmatrix} ^-1 & 10 \\ 16 & ^-2 \end{bmatrix}$

15. The table below shows the ages of 30 tennis players in a teen tournament.

Age	Frequency
19	6
18	6
17	12
16	4
15	2

Which statement is true?

A median > mode

B median = mode

C median < mode

D median > mean

16. There are 30 students in a class. The mean grade for that class on a test was computed as 80, but two students' grades were read incorrectly as 90 instead of 50. What will the average grade (rounded to the nearest tenth) be when it is recomputed using the correct scores?

17. Winter Spring bottled water comes in three sizes:

   6-pack of 0.5-liter bottles at $3.59 per 6-pack

   1-liter bottles at $0.99 each

   1.5-liter bottles at $1.59 each

If you need 9 liters of bottled water, how much would you save by buying 1.5-liter bottles instead of 6-packs of 0.5-liter bottles?

18. The two spinners shown have eight and four congruent sections respectively. If you spin each spinner once, what is the probability of obtaining the largest possible sum?

19. A craft store has orders to ship wreaths to 4 stores: Westwood Garden Center, Creative Gifts, Hands-On Crafts, Gifts for All. The wreaths come in three sizes: small, medium, and large. The given matrix shows the number of wreaths shipped to each store. Columns represent the four stores; rows represent the three sizes small, medium, and large respectively. If the small wreath sells for $18, medium for $24, and large for $40, what is the total amount billed to each store?

$$\begin{bmatrix} 4 & 6 & 0 & 5 \\ 5 & 3 & 3 & 5 \\ 2 & 1 & 6 & 5 \end{bmatrix}$$

20. For the local minor league baseball team, the ratio of games won to games played is 8 : 11. Write the ratio of games lost to games played.

21. You must walk 35 minutes to burn off the calories in one slice of cheese pizza. This is 1 minute less than 4 times the number of minutes it would take you to burn off the same number calories by running. How long would you have to run to burn the calories in one slice of cheese pizza?

22. You have a bag containing 2 oatmeal cookies and 2 chocolate-chip cookies. You randomly draw out 1 oatmeal cookie and eat it. What is the probability of randomly drawing another oatmeal cookie?

23. Justin's age next year will be twice what it was 10 years ago. Write an equation you could use to find out how old Justin is now.

24. Divide: $\dfrac{25a^5d^2}{5d}$

25. A baker wants to make a double batch of gingersnaps and half a batch of chocolate chip cookies. Each batch of gingersnaps requires $2\frac{1}{2}$ cups of sugar. Each batch of chocolate chip cookies requires $2\frac{3}{4}$ cups of sugar. A cup of sugar weighs 7 ounces. To the nearest half-pound, how many pounds of sugar will the baker need?

26. These are tests scores in Mme. Dubin's French class:

93, 92, 84, 81, 68, 81, 78, 77, 84, 63, 62, 90

- Construct a line plot for the data.
- State the median score for the data.
- What would happen to the median if one point were added to each of the test scores? Explain.

27. A package of gum has a price increase from $0.50 to $0.60. At the old price, a package contained 10 sticks of gum; now a package contains 8 sticks. Determine the percent increase in going from the old situation to the new. Explain your procedure and thinking.

28. Kathryn invests $2,000.00 for six years at 10% interest compounded annually. After the first three years, Elizabeth invests $3,000.00 for three years at 5% interest compounded annually. At the end of the six years, who would have more money? Explain.

29. On the first six tests in her social studies course, Jerelyn's scores were 92, 78, 86, 92, 95, and 90. Determine the median and the mode of her scores. If Jerelyn took a seventh test and raised the median of her scores exactly 1 point, what was her score on the seventh test?

30. A sweatshirt that usually costs $39.95 is on sale at a 15 percent discount. The sales tax is 6 percent. Find to the nearest cent:

- amount of the discount
- new price
- total cost including tax

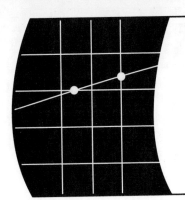

Chapter 4:
Patterns, and Functions

 PATTERNS

In a number of applications, problems can be solved by discovering a pattern and using the pattern to draw different conclusions. The pattern might be numerical or visual.

Computational Patterns

Many numerical situations involve patterns.
Examples:

a. repeating decimal

$$\frac{1}{11} = 0.0909$$

b. equivalent fractions

$$\frac{1}{2} = \frac{2}{4} = \frac{3}{6} = \frac{4}{8}$$

c. powers of ten
$$10^1 = 10$$
$$10^2 = 100$$
$$10^3 = 1,000$$
$$\vdots$$
$$10^9 = 1,000,000,000$$

d. concept of percent
$$1\% = \frac{1}{100}$$
$$10\% = \frac{10}{100}$$
$$50\% = \frac{50}{100}$$
$$100\% = \frac{100}{100}$$

e. multiplication pattern
$$9 \times 1 = 9$$
$$9 \times 2 = 18$$
$$9 \times 3 = 27$$
$$9 \times 4 = 36$$
$$9 \times 5 = 45$$
$$9 \times 6 = 54$$
$$9 \times 7 = 63$$
$$9 \times 8 = 72$$
$$9 \times 9 = 81$$

MODEL PROBLEMS

1. What is the units digit in the number equivalent of 3^{24}?

Solution: Since it is not convenient to compute the value of 3^{24}, you need to see if a pattern exists by examining small powers of 3.

$$\left.\begin{array}{l} 3^1 = 3 \\ 3^2 = 9 \\ 3^3 = 27 \\ 3^4 = 81 \end{array}\right\}$$ For the first four powers of 3, the units digits are different (namely, 3, 9, 7, 1).

$$\begin{array}{l} 3^5 = 243 \\ 3^6 = 729 \\ 3^7 = ..7 \\ 3^8 = ..1 \end{array}$$ Then the units digit begins to repeat. Assume that the pattern for the units digit continues as 3, 9, 7, 1. Note that this pattern is in groups of 4. You may conclude that every power of 3 that is a multiple of 4 will have a units digit of 1.

Answer: Since 3^{24} is a power of 3 that is a multiple of 4, the value of 3^{24} will have a units digit of 1.

2. In the decimal representation for $\dfrac{5}{33}$, what digit would be in the 30th decimal place?

Solution: The decimal representation for $\dfrac{5}{33}$ is 0.15151515.... Notice that in the repeating pattern, a 1 is in every odd position and a 5 is in every even position.

Answer: The digit in the 30th decimal place would be a 5.

Visual Patterns

Patterns often occur in diagrams and through visualization.
Example:

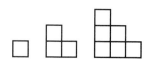

Visualizing this pattern shows that the next term is generated by adding a row of squares one greater in length than the bottom row of the previous term.

Visual patterns are often found in flooring, wallpaper, wrapping paper, store displays, and fabric.

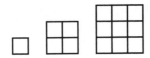

MODEL PROBLEM

How many unit squares are needed to represent the fifth term of the following pattern?

Solution:

METHOD 1: concrete

Notice that the first term is a 1 × 1 square, the second term is a 2 × 2 square, and the third term is a 3 × 3 square. Then, build the fourth term (4 × 4) and the fifth term (5 × 5).

Answer: Counting the unit squares in the fifth term produces a result of 25 unit squares.

METHOD 2: converting to a numerical pattern

Analyzing the number of unit squares used to build the three given terms produces the numerical pattern 1, 4, 9. Recognizing these numbers as consecutive perfect squares, you realize that the fifth term would have to be the fifth square, or 25.

Answer: 25 unit squares

Patterns can be formed by rotating or turning an object. A figure will be turned either clockwise or counterclockwise. The figures below show an object being turned 90° clockwise and 90° counterclockwise.

90° clockwise

90° counterclockwise

The pattern below shows a floor tile that has been moved in different positions.

Which of the following best describes the movement of the tile?

A flipped vertically
B flipped horizontally
C turned clockwise 90°
D turned counterclockwise 90°

Solution:

By observing the pattern it can be seen that the floor tile is being turned counterclockwise 90°.

Answer: D

PRACTICE

1. What is the units digit in 2^{40}?

   A 2 　　**B** 4 　　**C** 6 　　**D** 8

2. Which one of the following bases does NOT produce the same units digit when raised to any whole-number power?

   F 10 　　**G** 9 　　**H** 6 　　**J** 5

3. Which of the following would yield a repeating decimal pattern?

   A $\frac{1}{6}$ 　　**B** $\frac{1}{4}$ 　　**C** $\frac{3}{16}$ 　　**D** $\frac{1}{25}$

4. What digit is in the 45th decimal place in the decimal value of $\frac{7}{11}$?

   F 1 　　**G** 3 　　**H** 6 　　**J** 7

5. Terrence decides he is going to start saving pennies in a large plastic jar he has found. On Monday, he puts 1 cent into the jar. On Tuesday, he doubles the amount to 2 cents. On each succeeding day, he doubles the number of pennies he put in the day before. How many days will it take Terrence to save at least $20?

   A 11 　　**B** 12 　　**C** 15 　　**D** 26

6. Which of the following decimals shows a pattern equivalent to the visual pattern below?

   ⊢ T ⊣ ⊥ ⊢ T ⊣ ⊥

   F .12891289 . . . 　　**H** .541541541 . . .
   G .313131 . . . 　　**J** .7777 . . .

7. Analyze the pattern:

   PENCILPENCILPENCIL . . .

   If the pattern is continued, what letter will be in the 83rd position?

   A P 　　**B** E 　　**C** I 　　**D** L

8. Juan and Kim started a debating club. It was decided that once a month each member would debate every member of the club. It was also decided to add 1 new member to the club each month. Which of the following patterns could be used to determine the total number of debates in the fifth month the club was operating?

F 2, 6, 12, 20, 30   H 1, 3, 6, 10, 15
G 1, 4, 9, 16, 25   J 2, 3, 4, 5, 6

9. If the pattern below continues until all letters of the alphabet are shown, how many letters, including repetitions, will precede the last Z?

ABBCCCDDDD

10. How many dots are needed to represent the first five terms, in total, for the given sequence?

11. Given that: $\frac{1}{2} + \frac{1}{4} = \frac{3}{4}$

$$\frac{1}{2} + \frac{1}{4} + \frac{1}{8} = \frac{7}{8}$$

$$\frac{1}{2} + \frac{1}{4} + \frac{1}{8} + \frac{1}{16} = \frac{15}{16}$$

Find: $\frac{1}{2} + \frac{1}{4} + \frac{1}{8} + \frac{1}{16} + \frac{1}{32}$

12. A local restaurant has small tables that seat 4 people, one on each side. When the restaurant must seat larger groups of people, tables are put together so that they share a common side. When 2 tables are put together, 6 people can be seated. If 5 tables are put together into a long row, how many people can be seated?

13. Jared painted a 4 × 4 × 4 cube green on all 6 faces. When the paint dried, Jared cut the cube into 64 smaller cubes (1 × 1 × 1). If Jared looked at each small cube, how many would have green paint on exactly 2 faces? In completing this problem, discuss cases involving a smaller original cube in order to show a pattern to use to answer the question.

14. Mary notices that on a 2 × 2 checkerboard there are 5 squares of various sizes.

 This 2 × 2 board has four 1 × 1 squares and one 2 × 2 square.

Mary thinks that a 4 × 4 checkerboard would have twice as many squares. Do you agree or disagree with Mary's idea? Explain your reasoning.

15. For the given sequence, determine the total number of squares needed to represent the fifth term.

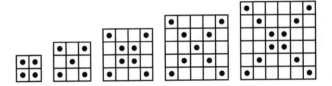

16. If the pattern is continued, how many dots would be in the 20th diagram?

17. The pattern below shows a puzzle piece that has been moved in different positions.

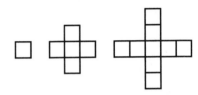

According to this pattern, what is the next position and what best describes the movement?

18. Suppose this pattern is continued. On the eighth figure, what percent of the figure is shaded? Explain your thought process.

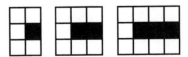

A *sequence* is a list of numbers in a particular order that follows a pattern. A *series* is the sum of the terms of a sequence.

Arithmetic Sequences

An *arithmetic sequence* has a *common difference* between two consecutive terms.

Example: 5,   8,   11,   14,   17, . . .

         3   3   3   3   common difference = 3

The next term is $17 + 3 = 20$.

MODEL PROBLEMS

1. Which of these are arithmetic sequences?

    I. 9, 15, 21, 27, 33, . . .

    II. 18, 10, 2, ⁻6, ⁻14, . . .

    III. 7, 11, 16, 22, 29, . . .

Solution: Check for a common difference.

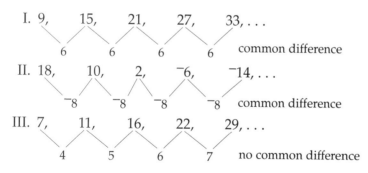

    I. 9,   15,   21,   27,   33, . . .

           6   6   6   6   common difference

    II. 18,   10,   2,   ⁻6,   ⁻14, . . .

           ⁻8   ⁻8   ⁻8   ⁻8   common difference

    III. 7,   11,   16,   22,   29, . . .

           4   5   6   7   no common difference

Answer: I and II are arithmetic sequences.

2. Find the 50th term of the arithmetic sequence:

$$3, 7, 11, 15, 19, 23, . . .$$

Solution: To find a particular term in an arithmetic sequence use the following formula: $a_n = a_1 + (n - 1)d$, **where n = term number and d = the common difference.** To find the 50th term, $n = 50$, $d = 7 - 3 = 4$, and $a_1 = 3$. By substituting into the formula you get:

$$a_n = a_1 + (n - 1)d$$
$$a_{50} = 3 + (50 - 1)4$$
$$a_{50} = 3 + 49 \cdot 4 = 199$$

Answer: The 50th term is 199.

Geometric Sequences

A *geometric sequence* has a *common ratio* between two consecutive terms.
Example: 2, 6, 18, 54, 162, . . .

$$\frac{6}{2} = 3, \frac{18}{6} = 3, \frac{54}{18} = 3, \frac{162}{54} = 3 \quad \text{common ratio} = 3$$

The next term is $162 \times 3 = 486$.

MODEL PROBLEMS

1. Which of these are geometric sequences?

  I. 16, 8, 4, 2, 1, . . .
  II. 10, 20, 80, 640, . . .
  III. 10, 50, 250, 1,250, . . .

Solution: Check for a common ratio.

  I. 16, 8, 4, 2, 1, . . .

$$\frac{8}{16} = \frac{1}{2}, \frac{4}{8} = \frac{1}{2}, \frac{2}{4} = \frac{1}{2} \quad \text{common ratio} = \frac{1}{2}$$

  II. 10, 20, 80, 640, . . .

$$\frac{20}{10} = 2, \frac{80}{20} = 4 \quad \text{no common ratio}$$

  III. 10, 50, 250, 1,250, . . .

$$\frac{50}{10} = 5, \frac{250}{50} = 5, \frac{1,250}{250} = 5 \quad \text{common ratio} = 5$$

Answer: I and III are geometric sequences.

2. Find the 10th term of the geometric sequence:

$$\frac{1}{2}, 1, 2, 4, 8, . . .$$

Solution: To find a particular term in a geometric sequence you can use the following formula: $a_n = a_1 \cdot r^{n-1}$, **where r is the common ratio and n is the term number.**

For the given problem, $n = 10$, $r = 1 \div \frac{1}{2} = 2$, $a_1 = \frac{1}{2}$.

Using the formula and substituting the appropriate values gives:

$$a_{10} = \frac{1}{2} \cdot 2^{(10-1)} = \frac{1}{2} \cdot 2^9 = 256$$

Answer: The 10th term of the sequence is 256.

Note: 2^9 can be evaluated using the $\boxed{y^x}$ key on a calculator.

Fibonacci Sequence

The *Fibonacci Sequence* is generated by adding the two previous terms to form the next term.

$$1, \quad 1, \quad \underset{(1+1)}{2,} \quad \underset{(1+2)}{3,} \quad \underset{(2+3)}{5,} \quad \underset{(3+5)}{8,} . . .$$

MODEL PROBLEM

Given the Fibonacci sequence 1, 1, 2, 3, 5, 8, . . . Answer the following.

- What is the 10th term of the sequence?
- What is the sum of the first 10 terms?

Solution:

- To determine the 10th term, extend the sequence using the rule "add the two previous terms to form the next term."

Answer: 1, 1, 2, 3, 5, 8, 13, 21, 34, 55

- To find the sum, add the 10 given numbers.

$$1 + 1 + 2 + 3 + 5 + 8 + 13 + 21 + 34 + 55 = 143$$

Answer: The sum of the 10 terms is 143.

Arithmetic Series

The sum of the first n terms of an arithmetic sequence is given by the formula:

$$S_n = n\left(\frac{a_1 + a_n}{2}\right) \quad \text{where } a_1 = \text{first term}$$
$$a_n = n\text{th term}$$

MODEL PROBLEM

For the arithmetic series $5 + 7 + 9 + \ldots + 99 + 101$ compute the sum.

Solution: Use the formula $S_n = n\left(\frac{a_1 + a_n}{2}\right)$, where $a_1 = 5$ and $a_n = 101$.

To find n use the arithmetic sequence formula.

$$a_n = a_1 + (n - 1)d \quad a_1 = 5, a_n = 101, d = 2$$
$$101 = 5 + (n - 1)2$$
$$96 = 2(n - 1)$$
$$48 = n - 1$$
$$49 = n$$

Therefore, $S_n = 49\left(\frac{5 + 101}{2}\right) = 49\left(\frac{106}{2}\right) = 49 \cdot 53 = 2{,}597$

Geometric Series

The sum of the first n terms of a geometric sequence is given by the formula:

$$S_n = \frac{a_1(r^n - 1)}{r - 1}$$

where a_1 = first term

n = term number

r = common ratio

MODEL PROBLEM

For the geometric series $3 + 6 + 12 + \ldots$ compute the sum of the first 10 terms.

Solution: Using the formula

$$S_n = \frac{a_1(r^n - 1)}{r - 1}$$ where $a_1 = 3$, $n = 10$, $r = 2$

$$S_n = \frac{3(2^{10} - 1)}{2 - 1} = \frac{3(1{,}024 - 1)}{1} = \frac{3(1{,}023)}{1} = 3{,}069$$

Infinite Geometric Series

When the absolute value of the ratio in a geometric sequence is greater than 1 the sequence *diverges,* and as a result there is no limit or sum for an infinite number of terms. However, when the absolute value of the ratio is less than 1 the sequence *converges,* and there is a limit or sum that can be obtained.

For example: (1) $5 + 15 + 45 + 135 + \ldots$ has no limit or sum for an infinite number of terms since $r = 3$.

(2) $\dfrac{1}{2} + \dfrac{1}{4} + \dfrac{1}{8} + \dfrac{1}{16} + \ldots$ has a limit because $r = \dfrac{1}{2}$.

The sum of the infinite series is 1.

The formula for an infinite geometric series where the absolute value of $r < 1$

is $S = \dfrac{a_1}{1 - r}$, where a_1 = first term and r = common ratio.

MODEL PROBLEM

Find the sum: $1 + \dfrac{1}{3} + \dfrac{1}{9} + \dfrac{1}{27} + \ldots$

Solution: $r = \dfrac{1}{3}, a_1 = 1$

$$S = \frac{a_1}{1 - r}$$

$$S = \frac{1}{1 - \dfrac{1}{3}} = \frac{1}{\dfrac{2}{3}} = \frac{3}{2}$$

Answer: $\dfrac{3}{2}$ is the sum or limit for the series.

PRACTICE

1. Which of the following is a geometric sequence?

   A $6, 7\dfrac{1}{3}, 8\dfrac{2}{3}, 9, \ldots$

   B $\dfrac{1}{2}, \dfrac{1}{3}, \dfrac{1}{4}, \dfrac{1}{5}, \ldots$

   C $^-10, ^-100, ^-1{,}000, \ldots$

   D $2, 4, 2, 4, 2, 4, \ldots$

2. Which of the following would give you the 20th term of the arithmetic sequence 6, 13, 20, 27, . . . ?

   F 20×6 **H** 20×7

   G $6 + 20 \times 7$ **J** $6 + 19 \times 7$

3. Which of the following is NOT an arithmetic sequence?

   A $2, 8, 32, 128, \ldots$ **C** $10, 10, 10, 10, \ldots$

   B $\dfrac{1}{2}, \dfrac{3}{4}, 1, \dfrac{5}{4}, \ldots$ **D** $8, 4, 0, ^-4, \ldots$

4. Which of the following would NOT be a term of this geometric sequence?

   $$3, 6, 12, 24, \ldots$$

   F 48   **G** 64   **H** 96   **J** 192

5. Which is the next term in the given Fibonacci sequence?

   $$1, 1, 2, 3, 5, 8, \ldots$$

   A 11   **B** 13   **C** 16   **D** 40

6. Which of these sequences is a Fibonacci-like sequence?

   F $1, 4, 5, 9, 14, 23, \ldots$

   G $1, 4, 4, 16, 64, \ldots$

   H $1, 4, 9, 16, 25, \ldots$

   J $1, 4, 8, 12, 16, \ldots$

7. The sum of the arithmetic series $^-27 + ^-17 + ^-7 + \ldots + 43$ is

   A 32   **B** 64   **C** 128   **D** 280

8. The sum of the first 10 terms of the geometric series $1 + 2 + 4 + 8 + 16 + \ldots$ is

   F 128 **G** 255 **H** 512 **J** 1,023

9. The sum of the infinite series $1 + \dfrac{1}{4} + \dfrac{1}{16} + \ldots$ is

   A $\dfrac{1}{4}$ **B** $\dfrac{3}{4}$ **C** $\dfrac{4}{3}$ **D** 4

10. For which of the following is it possible to find the sum?

   F $\dfrac{1}{2} + \dfrac{1}{3} + \dfrac{1}{4} + \dfrac{1}{5} + \dfrac{1}{6} + \ldots$

   G $\dfrac{1}{2} + \dfrac{1}{2} + \dfrac{1}{2} + \dfrac{1}{2} + \dfrac{1}{2} + \ldots$

   H $\dfrac{1}{2} - \dfrac{1}{4} + \dfrac{1}{8} - \dfrac{1}{16} + \ldots$

   J $\dfrac{1}{2} + 1 + 2 + 4 + \ldots$

11. A special sequence is formed by taking twice the sum of the two previous terms to find the third term and all succeeding terms. If the first four terms are 1, 2, 6, 16, find the 8th term.

12. In an arithmetic sequence, the 5th term is 23 and the 7th term is 33. Find the common difference for the sequence.

13. The first four terms of an arithmetic sequence are 2, 8, 14, 20, and 122 is the 21st term. What is the value of the 20th term?

14. In this geometric sequence, what is the common ratio? $81, 27, 9, 3, \ldots$

15. If the 9th term of an arithmetic sequence is 100 and the 10th term is 111, find the value of the first term.

16. Create an arithmetic sequence of at least six terms for which the common difference is $^-3$. Explain why the sequence you wrote is arithmetic. Also explain why there would be an infinite number of possible sequences fitting the given condition.

17. A tennis ball hit in the air 27 feet rebounds to two-thirds of its previous height after each bounce. Find the total vertical distance (up and down) the ball has traveled when it hits the ground the tenth time.

18. A small business had sales of $50,000 during its first year of operation. If the sales increase by $6,000 per year, what is its total sales in its eleventh year?

19. The number of bacteria in a culture triples every four hours. If 1,000 bacteria are present initially, how many bacteria will be present at the end of 24 hours?

20. A machine's value depreciates annually at a rate of 30% of the value it had at the beginning of that year. If its initial value is $10,000, find its value at the end of the eighth year.

The relationship "The perimeter of a square depends on the length of a side" can be expressed in a variety of ways.

a. Verbal statement: The perimeter of a square is four times the length of a side.

b. Table of values:

Side Length	Perimeter
1	4
2	8
3	12
4	16

c. Set of ordered pairs: {(1, 4), (2, 8), (3, 12), (4, 16)}

d. Equation: $P = 4s$, where s is the length of a side of the square and P is the perimeter.

e. Graph: Plot the table of values to obtain the graph.

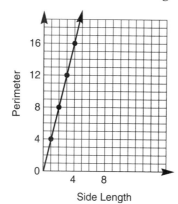

MODEL PROBLEM

A can of soda costs $0.75. The amount of money you spend on soda is related to the number of cans you purchase. Show the relationship as a table of values containing 5 sets of values and write an equation to summarize the relationship.

Solution: Table of values

Number of Cans	Cost
1	$0.75
2	$1.50
3	$2.25
4	$3.00
5	$3.75

Equation: To obtain the cost (C), multiply the number of cans by the cost of one can.

$$C = 0.75n, \text{ where } n \text{ is the number of cans.}$$

 PRACTICE

1. This table indicates a linear relationship between x and y.

x	1	3	5	7	9
y	1	7	13	?	25

According to this pattern, which number is missing from the table?

A 15   **B** 19   **C** 21   **D** 23

2. A plumber charges $48 for each hour she works plus an additional service charge of $25. At this rate, how much would the plumber charge for a job that took 4.5 hours?

3. The cost of a long-distance telephone call can be computed based on the following formula:

$T = C + nr$, where T = total cost of the call in dollars

C = charge for the first three minutes in dollars

n = number of additional minutes the call lasts

r = rate per minute for each additional minute in dollars

What is the cost of a 15-minute long-distance call if a person is charged $1.75 for the first three minutes and $0.15 for each additional minute?

4. A local parking lot charges $1.75 for the first hour and $1.25 for each additional hour or part of an hour. Represent the relationship of parking charges to hours parked:

- in a table of values for 1 to 6 hours.
- in an equation in which t represents time parked in hours and C the total cost of parking.
- as a graph with hours parked on the horizontal and total cost on the vertical.

4.4 RELATIONS AND FUNCTIONS

Recall that the formula for the circumference of a circle is $C = \pi d$. The circumference *depends* on the length of the diameter. The length of the diameter is the **independent variable** and the circumference is the **dependent variable**. Another way to express the relationship is to say "circumference is a **function** of diameter." For different values of d, the function can be displayed by a table, set of ordered pairs, equation, or graph.

a. **Table**

d	1	2	3	4
C	3.14	6.28	9.42	12.56

(d and C in inches)

b. **Set of ordered pairs**

$\{(1, 3.14), (2, 6.28), (3, 9.42), (4, 12.56), \ldots\}$

c. **Equation**

$$C = \pi d$$

d. **Graph**

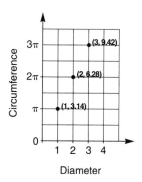

A set of ordered pairs is called a **relation.** The example above shows that circumference and diameter constitute a relation. One can observe that for any specified value for the diameter, there can be only one resulting value for the circumference. A relation with this property is called a **function.**

When a relation is listed as a set of ordered pairs, a function exists when for every x-value (first coordinate) there is only one y-value (second coordinate).

Which of the following is NOT a function?

    A $(^-1, 5), (1, 4), (5, 3), (0, 6)$
    B $(2, 4), (4, 8), (9, 18)$
    C $(3, 0), (3, 1), (3, 2), (3, 3)$
    D $(9, 0), (7, 0), (^-5, 0), (13, 0)$

Solution: To be a function a given set of ordered pairs must be such that for every value of x there is only one value for y. In choice **C**, 3 is repeated for x with four different y-values. Hence, **C** is not a function.

The *domain* of a function is all the possible x-values of the points on the graph. The *range* of a function is all the possible y-values on the graph. The *zeros* or roots of a function are the x-values where the graph crosses the x-axis. The *maximum* and *minimum* values of a function are the highest and lowest y-values, respectively, on the graph.

In a function the values for the independent variable are considered as the input or domain; the values for the dependent variable are considered output or range. For the function $y = 2x$, if the domain is the set of whole numbers, the output or range would be the set of even whole numbers.

$$\nearrow \overset{y = 2x}{} \nwarrow$$

dependent   independent
variable,   variable,
output   input

Consider the following relations displayed as graphs:

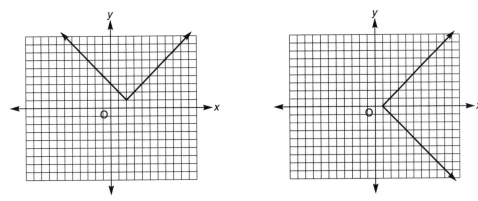

The one on the left is a function, while the one on the right is not. In the graph on the left, one can observe a unique value for y for each value of x considered. In contrast, the graph on the right has two different values for y for given values of x. This distinction can be visualized through a technique known as the vertical line test.

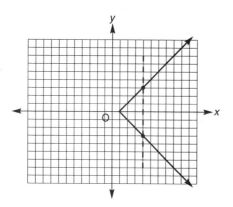

If the vertical line passes through a graph more than once, the graph is not the graph of a function.

Consider the following nonlinear function.

Equation: $y = x^2 + 3$

Table of values: Set of ordered pairs: $\{(0, 3), (1, 4), (^-1, 4), (2, 7), (^-2, 7) \ldots\}$

x	y
0	3
1	4
$^-1$	4
2	7
$^-2$	7

Graph:

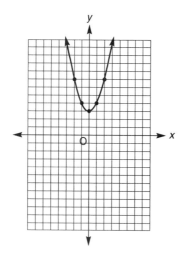

In this example, y is clearly a function of x. For any given value of x the value of y is found by adding 3 to the square of x. Since any value can be used for input, the domain of the function is the set of real numbers. Since the square of a real number must be nonnegative, the output values in this function must be 3 or greater. This means that the range is the set of real numbers greater than or equal to 3.

The following table summarizes some different types of functions.

Types of Functions	
Constant Function $y = 5$ $\{(^-2, 5), (^-1, 5), (0, 5) \ldots\}$	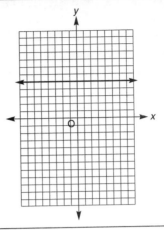
Linear Function $y = 2x + 1$ $\{(^-2, ^-3), (^-1, ^-1), (0, 1) \ldots\}$	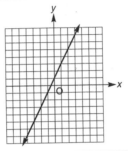
Quadratic Function $y = x^2$ $\{(^-2, 4), (^-1, 1), (0, 0) \ldots\}$	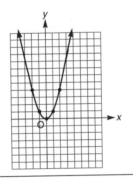
Absolute Value Function $y = |x|$ $\{(^-2, 2), (^-1, 1), (0, 0), (1, 1), (2, 2) \ldots\}$	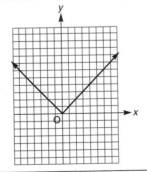
Exponential Function $y = 2^x$ $\{(^-2, 0.25), (^-1, 0.5), (0, 1), (1, 2), (2, 4) \ldots\}$	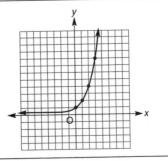

An alternative notation used for functions is referred to as $f(x)$ (read as "f of x" or "f at x").

$$\text{Given } y = x^2 + 3 \qquad f(x) = x^2 + 3$$

For this function, $f(4) = 4^2 + 3 = 19$ and $f(^-2) = (^-2)^2 + 3 = 7$.

Formulas can often be expressed using function notation. For example, the formula for the perimeter of a square can be expressed as $p(s) = 4s$; perimeter of a square is a function of side length.

Greatest-Integer Function

Consider a function in which:

$y = ^-2$ when $^-2 \leq x < ^-1$

$y = ^-1$ when $^-1 \leq x < 0$

$y = 0$ when $0 \leq x < 1$

$y = 1$ when $1 \leq x < 2$

$y = 2$ when $2 \leq x < 3$

This function is called the ***greatest-integer function*** (notation $y = \lfloor x \rfloor$) since for any real number x in the domain, the function gives the greatest integer less than or equal to the domain value. For example:

$$\lfloor 4.2 \rfloor = 4; \lfloor 4.99 \rfloor = 4; \lfloor 5 \rfloor = 5; \lfloor 0.001 \rfloor = 0; \lfloor ^-4.1 \rfloor = ^-5; \lfloor \pi \rfloor = 3$$

The ***least-integer function*** is a similar function that gives the least integer greater than or equal to the domain value. For example:

$$\lceil 4.2 \rceil = 5; \lceil 4.99 \rceil = 5; \lceil 5 \rceil = 5; \lceil 0.001 \rceil = 1; \lceil ^-4.1 \rceil = ^-4; \lceil \pi \rceil = 4$$

The graphs of these functions are called step functions:

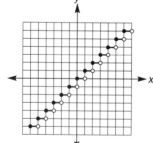

Greatest-Integer Function

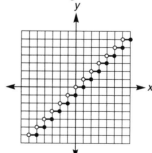

Least-Integer Function

First class postal rates are an example of a real-world situation that can be represented by a least-integer function.

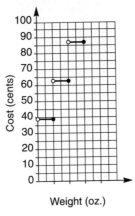

Weight (oz.)

$$C = 39 + 24\lceil w - 1 \rceil$$

where C = postage charge in cents

w = weight of the envelope in ounces

Note: the domain would contain only values for w that are greater than 0.

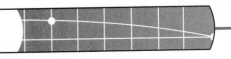

MODEL PROBLEMS

1. In a parking lot, the charges are $3.00 for the first hour (or any part of the hour) and $1.00 for every additional hour (or part of the hour). Answer the following.

   - How much would the charge be for 4 hours and 20 minutes?
   - Explain why the graph of parking charges as a function of time would be a step function.
   - Graph the function the step function.

Solution:
   - 4 hours and 20 minutes would be the same charge as 5 hours. With $3.00 for the first hour and 4 hours at $1.00 per hour, the final charge would be $7.00.
   - The graph would be a least-integer function because you have an interval of values for time yielding the same total parking charge. For example, anything over 1 hour but not more than 2 hours would have a charge of $4.00; anything over 2 hours but not more than 3 hours would have a charge of $5.00, etc.
   -

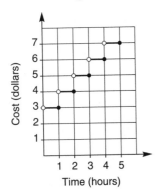

Time (hours)

2. What is the value of y when $x = 5$?

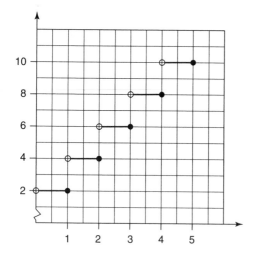

   A 4
   B 8
   C 10
   D 12

Solution: By observing the graph of the step function, the value of y when x is 5 is 10.

Answer: C

1. Which of the following sets of ordered pairs does NOT represent a function?

   A {($^-$2, 2), (2, 2), ($^-$5, 5), (5, 5)}
   B {(7, 5), (8, 5), ($^-$8, 5), ($^-$7, 5)}
   C {(2, 3), (2, 4), (2, 5), (2, 6)}
   D {(1, 1), (2, 8), (3, 27), (4, 64)}

2. If the volume of a cube is a function of the length of an edge, which of the following equations represents the situation?

   F $V = 3e$
   G $V = e^3$
   H $V = e + 3$
   J $V = \sqrt[3]{e}$

3. A function is described by the equation $R = 2t + 3$. What value for R is missing from the table?

t	1	2	3	...	10
R	5	7	9	...	?

   A 11   **B** 15   **C** 23   **D** 26

4. Look at the graphs below.

   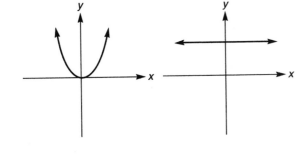

   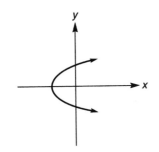

Using the graphs, which of the following statements is true?

   F Graphs I, II, and III represent functions.
   G Graphs I and II represent functions.
   H Only graph II is a function.
   J Graphs II and III are functions.

5. If $f(x) = 3^x - 2^x$, what is the value of $f(^-2)$?

   A $\dfrac{1}{5}$ **B** $\dfrac{5}{36}$ **C** $\dfrac{^-5}{36}$ **D** $^-2$

6. Which of the following tables would be a reasonable representation for the relationship between the price (P) of an item and the sales tax (T) for that item?

   F

P	T
2.00	0.12
6.00	0.12
15.50	0.12
85.00	0.12

   H

P	T
2.00	0.12
6.00	0.36
15.50	0.93
85.00	5.10

   G

P	T
2.00	0.48
6.00	0.36
15.50	0.24
85.00	0.12

   J

P	T
2.00	0.12
6.00	0.14
15.50	0.24
85.00	0.12

7. This graph illustrates a constant function:

   Which of the following is a situation that can be modeled by a constant function?

   A The number of cars at a parkway tollbooth during the day
   B The ratio of the circumferences of various circles to the lengths of their diameters
   C Your heart rate during a 20-minute exercise period
   D The value of a car over a 10-year period

8. The given table is generated from which of the following rules?

x	⁻2	⁻1	0	1	2
$f(x)$	⁻2	⁻3	⁻4	⁻5	⁻6

F $f(x) = 2x + 2$ **H** $f(x) = x + 4$
G $f(x) = {}^-4 - x$ **J** $f(x) = {}^-3x$

9. What is the range of the function $y = x^2 + 1$ when the domain is $\{0, 2, 4\}$?

A $\{1, 3, 5\}$ **C** $\{1, 9, 25\}$
B $\{1, 5, 9\}$ **D** $\{1, 5, 17\}$

10. If $f(x) = 2^x$, what is the value of $f(10) - f(6)$?

F 4   **G** 64   **H** 512   **J** 960

11. Carol purchases an appliance on an installment plan. She pays $50 a month until the appliance is paid off. Which of the following graphs matches the relationship between months and the unpaid balance?

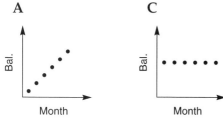

A

C

B

D

12. The functions $y = 3x$ and $y = 3^x$ represent very different relationships. If you take $x = 4$ from the domain of each, how many times larger is the range value for $y = 3^x$ than for $y = 3x$?

F They are equal.   **H** $\dfrac{4}{27}$
G 6.75   **J** 5.33

13. The given graph shows the linear function $y = 2x + k$ $(k > 0)$.

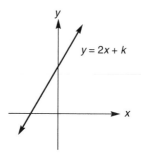

Based on the graph, which of the following must be true about the solution to the equation $2x + k = 0$ $(k > 0)$?

A There is no solution.
B The solution is approximately $x = 3$.
C There is one negative real number solution.
D There are two solutions, one positive and one negative.

14. Look at the graph below.

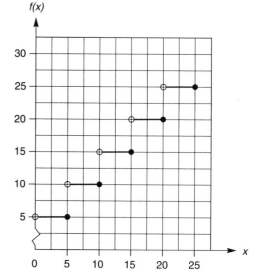

What is the value of $f(x)$ when $x = 25$?

F 15
G 20
H 25
J 30

15. This graph illustrates a step function:

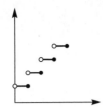

Which of the following applications could NOT be represented by the graph?

A Postage rates per ounce
B Charges at a parking lot per hour
C Taxicab fare compared to distance
D Temperature over the course of an afternoon

16. Karen and Samantha were looking at the table showing selected Maryland towns and cities with their zip codes.

Town or City	Zip Code
Saint Charles	20604
Waldorf	20604
Cobb Island	20625
Faulkner	20632
Rockville	20847
Rockville	20848
Rockville	20849

The two girls agreed that the relationship of town or city to zip code was not an example of a function. Karen said the Saint Charles/Waldorf example was the reason. However, Samantha said that it was the Rockville example that resulted in it not being a function. Who is correct? Explain your position.

17. The graph below displays a function: $y = f(x)$.

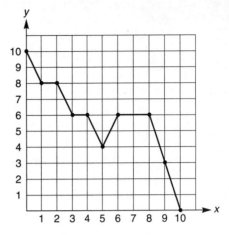

- What is the value of $f(1)$?
- What is the value of $f(6.73)$?
- What two values satisfy $f(x) = 4$?

4.5 SLOPE

Slope of a Line

Consider the linear function $y = 2x + 3$. By looking at a table of values, one can see that as the x-value increases by 1, the y-value always increases by 2. This means that there is a constant rate of change for the function. The rate of change is called the *slope*. This can also be shown through the graph of the line associated with the function.

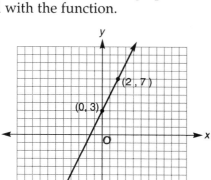

x	y
⁻1	1
0	3
1	5
2	7
3	9

If the coordinates of two points on the line are known, the slope can be found by using the formula

$$\text{slope} = \frac{\text{rise}}{\text{run}} = \frac{\text{change in } y}{\text{change in } x} = \frac{y_2 - y_1}{x_2 - x_1} = \frac{7 - 3}{2 - 0} = \frac{4}{2} = 2$$

Lines with different types of slopes:

If a line is parallel to the x-axis, the line has no steepness. Its slope is zero.

If a line is parallel to the y-axis, the line has an undefined slope.

If a line rises from left to right, its slope is positive.

If a line falls from left to right, its slope is negative.

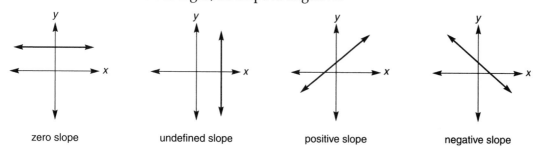

zero slope   undefined slope   positive slope   negative slope

A line passing through the points $(\mathbf{^-}3, 5)$ and $(5, y)$ has a slope of $\frac{1}{4}$. Find the value of y.

Solution:

$$\text{slope} = \frac{y_2 - y_1}{x_2 - x_1}$$

$$\frac{1}{4} = \frac{y - 5}{5 - (^-3)}$$

$$\frac{1}{4} = \frac{y - 5}{8}$$

$$4y - 20 = 8$$
$$4y = 28$$
$$y = 7$$

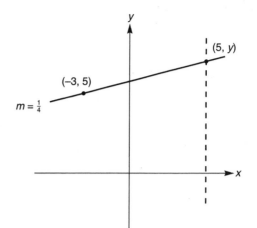

Slope-Intercept Form of the Equation of a Line

For the family of parallel lines shown, the lines have the same slope. However, note that each line crosses the y-axis at a different point. This point is known as the y-intercept. For the linear function, $y = 2x + 3$, when x is equal to zero, the value of y becomes 3. Hence, the ordered pair $(0, 3)$ becomes the y-intercept for the line.

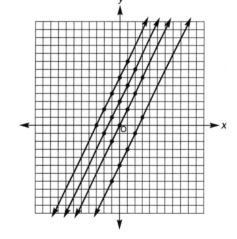

Slope-Intercept Form:	
$y = 2x + 3$	$y = mx + b$
↑ ↑	↑ ↑
slope y-intercept	slope y-intercept

Equation	Slope	y-intercept	Illustration
$y = {}^-3x - 1$	$m = {}^-3$	$b = {}^-1$	
$y = \dfrac{3}{4}x$	$m = \dfrac{3}{4}$	$b = 0$	
$y = 5$	$m = 0$	$b = 5$	

1. Find the equation for the graph below.

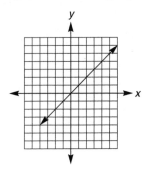

Solution:

Step 1: Find the slope m.

$$m = \frac{3 - 1}{3 - 1} = \frac{2}{2} = 1$$

The slope is 1.

Step 2: Locate a point (x_1, y_1) that the line passes through, lets use $(5, 5) = (x, y)$.

Step 3: Substitute all the known information into the slope-intercept form $y = mx + b$ and solve for b.

$m = 1$, point $(5, 5) = (x, y)$
$y = mx + b$
$5 = 1(5) + b$
$5 = 5 + b$
$0 = b$

Therefore, the equation of the line is $y = (1)x + 0$ or $y = x$. **Answer**

2. Find the equation of the line passing through the points $(^-2, 5)$ and $(6, 1)$.

Solution: In order to use slope-intercept form, first find the slope.

$$m = \frac{y_2 - y_1}{x_2 - x_1} = \frac{5 - 1}{^-2 - 6} = \frac{4}{^-8} = \frac{-1}{2}$$

The equation would be $y = \frac{-1}{2}x + b$. It is now necessary to find the value of b. Knowing that either given point satisfies the equation, one can substitute in the coordinates of either point in order to find b.

$$y = mx + b$$

$$y = \frac{-1}{2}x + b$$

Using $(6, 1)$ $1 = \left(\frac{-1}{2}\right)6 + b$

$1 = {^-3} + b$

$4 = b$ and the final equation is

$$y = \frac{-1}{2}x + 4$$

3. A small company makes a new type of container. A mathematician employed by the company claims that the total cost (in dollars) of producing n containers is given by the formula

$$C = 2n + 600$$

Graph this cost function and explain the significance of the slope and the y-intercept.

Solution: The y-intercept, $(0, 600)$, shows that the cost is $600 before any containers are produced. The slope, 2, indicates that the cost of producing each new container is $2.

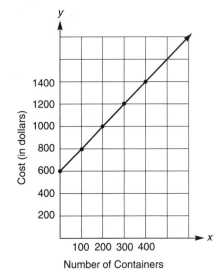

1. Which equation describes the graph below?

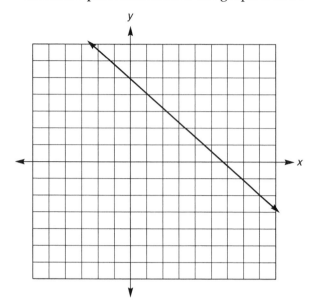

   A $y = {}^-5x + 30$
   B $y = 6x + 30$
   C $5x + 6y = 30$
   D $5y + 6y = 30$

2. Find the equation of the line containing the points $({}^-1, {}^-3)$ and $(0, 5)$.

   F $y = 8x$ **H** $y = 8x + 5$

   G $y = {}^-8x + 5$ **J** $y = \frac{1}{8}x + 5$

3. How many of the following lines have a slope of 2?

$$y = x + 2 \qquad y = 2x \qquad 2y = x$$
$$4y - 8x = 11 \qquad 8x - 4 = 7$$

   A 1   **B** 2   **C** 3   **D** 4

4. Write the equation, in slope-intercept form, for the line passing through $(8, 0)$ perpendicular to the line $y = 2x$.

   F $y = -\frac{1}{2}x + 8$ **H** $y = {}^-2x + 4$

   G $y = -\frac{1}{2}x + 4$ **J** $y = {}^-2x + 8$

5. Which equation describes the graph below?

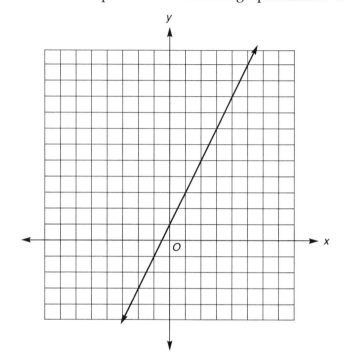

   A $y = x + 1$
   B $y = x + 2$
   C $y = 2(x + 1)$
   D $y = 2x + 1$

6. Which equation describes the graph below?

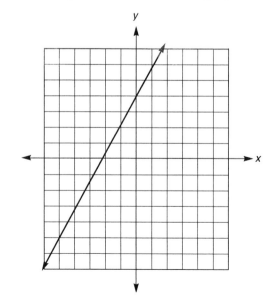

   F $y = {}^-2x + 4$ **H** $y = 2x + 4$
   G $y - 2x = {}^-4$ **J** $x = 2y + 4$

7. Which equation describes the graph below?

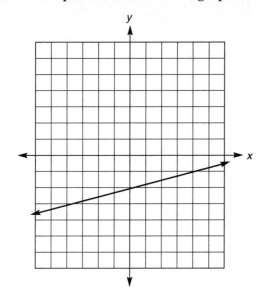

A $y = \frac{1}{4}x - 8$

B $y = \frac{1}{4}x - 2$

C $y = \frac{1}{4}x + 2$

D $y = 4x - 2$

8. Write an equation that describes the following graph.

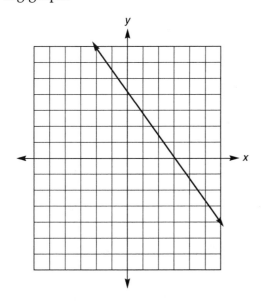

9. Write an equation that describes the following graph.

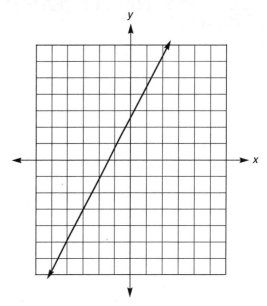

10. Brittany has a potted kudzu vine that is 10 inches long. As long as she waters it, it grows two inches each day.

- Explain why this situation is an example of linear change.
- Write an equation, in slope-intercept form, to represent the situation.
- Draw the resulting graph.
- If Brittany keeps watering the vine, when will it be 30 inches long? Show where this answer is on the graph.

4.6 Nonlinear Functions

A ***nonlinear function*** is one whose graph does not describe a straight line. In the tables shown below, $y = x^2$ and $y = 2^x$ are nonlinear functions.

x	$y = 3x + 1$
1	4
2	7
3	10
4	13
5	16

x	$y = x^2$
1	1
2	4
3	9
4	16
5	25

x	$y = 2^x$
1	2
2	4
3	8
4	16
5	32

In contrast with the linear function on the left ($y = 3x + 1$), the other two are examples of nonlinear functions. In these examples, you do not obtain a constant rate of change.

$$y = x^2$$

From (1, 1) to (2, 4) the rate of change is $\frac{4-1}{2-1} = \frac{3}{1} = 3$

From (2, 4) to (3, 9) the rate of change is $\frac{9-4}{3-2} = \frac{5}{1} = 5$

$$y = 2^x$$

From (1, 2) to (2, 4) the rate of change is $\frac{4-2}{2-1} = \frac{2}{1} = 2$

From (2, 4) to (3, 8) the rate of change is $\frac{8-4}{3-2} = \frac{4}{1} = 4$

Graphs of Nonlinear Functions

Since there is no constant rate of change for nonlinear functions its graph is a curve. The graph below is an example of a nonlinear function.

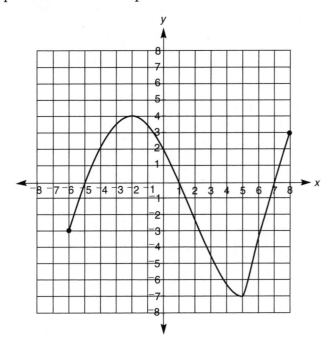

The general properties for the graph of a nonlinear function are the same for the graph of a linear function. The domain is for this example is $^-6 \leq x \leq 8$. The range is $^-7 \leq y \leq 4$.

Recall that the zeros of a function are the x-values where the graph crosses the x-axis. In the above graph, the zeros of this function are $x = {}^-5$ and $x = 7$.

The maximum value of a function is the y-value of the highest point on the graph. Graphically, the maximum value of a nonlinear function is shown as a *peak* on the curve. In our example, the maximum value is 4. The minimum value of a function is the y-value of the lowest point on the graph. Graphically, the minimum value of a nonlinear function is shown as a *valley* on the curve. In our example, the minimum value is $^-7$.

Look at the graph shown below.

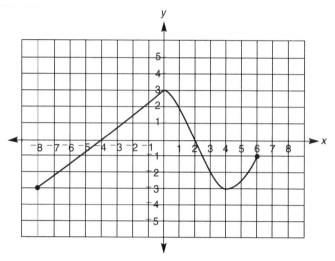

Answer the following:
- What is the domain and range of the function?
- What are the zeros of the function?
- What is the maximum and minimum of the function?

Solution:

- The domain of the function is $^-8 \leq x \leq 6$. The range of the function is $^-3 \leq y \leq 3$.
- The zeros of the function are at $x = {}^-4$ and at $x = 2$.
- The maximum of the function is 3 and the minimum of the function is $^-3$.

Continuity of a Function

Continuity is property of a function. A *continuous* function is a function whose graph can be drawn without lifting the pencil from the paper. A continuous function has no breaks or holes in its graph. For example, look at the graph below.

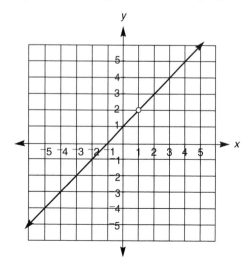

Since there is a hole in the graph when x is equal to 1, the function is not continuous at $x = 1$.

In a function, the point $x = a$ is called the *point of discontinuity* if the function is not continuous at that point. In the example above, $x = 1$ is the point of discontinuity.

Another type of discontinuity is shown below.

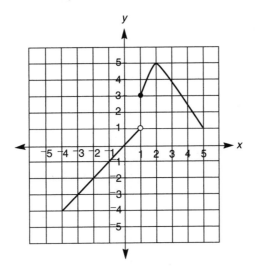

If the point (1, 3) is removed and replaced by (1, 1) to fill the gap, the function would be continuous. This type of discontinuity is called *removable discontinuity*.

MODEL PROBLEM

Look at the graph of the function below.

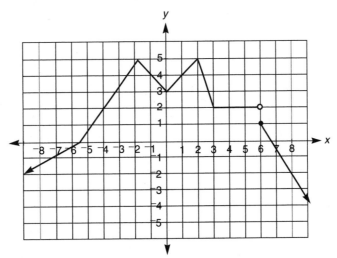

For what value of x is this function not continuous?

Solution:
There is a break in the function at $x = 6$. Therefore, the function is not continuous at $x = 6$.

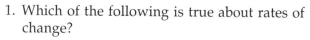

1. Which of the following is true about rates of change?

   A Rates of change are always constant.
   B A horizontal line has a rate of change of zero.
   C Two perpendicular lines have the same rate of change.
   D The line $y = 8x$ has the same rate of change as $y = {}^-8x$.

2. Look at the function that is graphed below.

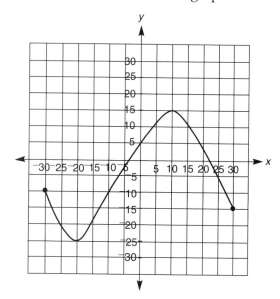

   What are the maximum and minimum values of this function?

   F maximum 10, minimum $^-20$
   G maximum 15, minimum $^-25$
   H maximum 20, minimum $^-30$
   J maximum 25, minimum $^-35$

3. Look at the graph below.

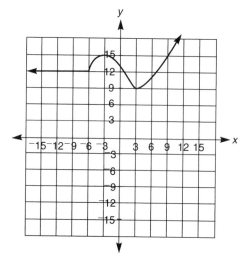

   Which of these terms does the y-coordinate of the point (3, 9) represent?

   A zero
   B intercept
   C minimum
   D maximum

4. Look at the function graphed below.

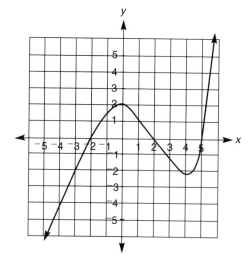

   Which of these represents the number of zeros of this function?

   F 3
   G 2
   H 1
   J 0

5. Look at the graph of the function below.

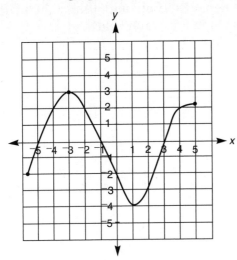

Which of the following statements is true about the function?

A The minimum value is 3.
B The minimum value is 5.
C The maximum value is 3.
D The maximum value is 5.

6. Look at the graph of the function below.

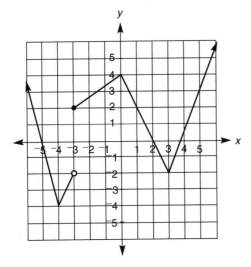

Which of the following is true about the function?

F The graph is not a function.
G The function is continuous at $x = 3$.
H The function is not continuous at $x = 3$.
J The function is not continuous at $x = {}^-3$.

7. Look at the graph of the function below.

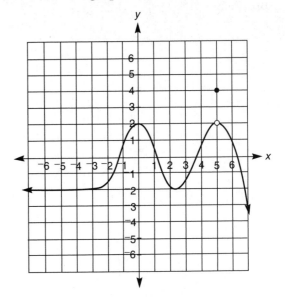

The function is not continuous at

A $x = 2$
B $x = 5$
C $y = 2$
D $y = 5$

8. Which of the following functions has a minimum value of 8?

F

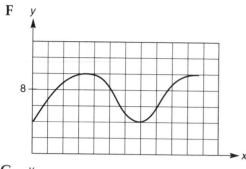

G

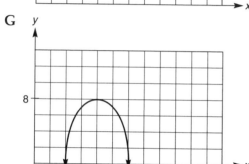

H

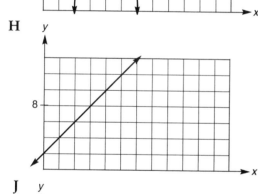

J

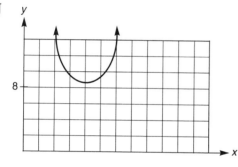

9. The relationship between the time a ball is thrown in the air and its height in feet is shown in the graph below.

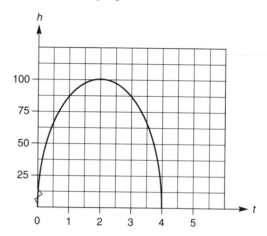

What does the y-coordinate in the ordered pair (2, 100) represent?

10. The graph of the function shown below has a maximum value when t equals

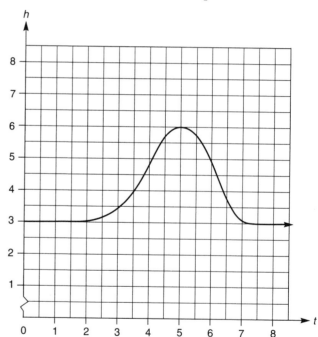

4.7 SOLVING SYSTEMS OF LINEAR EQUATIONS

Two or more linear equations with the same variables form a *system of linear equations*. A *solution* to a system is any pair of value (x, y) that makes all equations true. For example, the pair $(2, 4)$ means $x = 2$ and $y = 4$; $(2, 4)$ is a solution to the system of equations $y = 2x$ and $y = x + 2$.

There are two methods for solving systems of equations algebraically: the *addition-subtraction method* and the *substitution method*. Remember that the solution to a system of equations is a value for *each variable*, not just one.

To Solve Systems of Equations with the Addition-Subtraction Method

- If necessary, rewrite the equation in the form $ax + by = c$. This is the *standard form* of a linear equation.
- Decide which variable you want to eliminate.
- Multiply one or both equations by constants, if necessary, so that coefficients of the variable you want to eliminate are opposites.
- Set the equations up in columns. Align like terms.
- Add the columns. This will result in a single equation in one variable.
- Solve the resulting equation.
- Substitute the resulting value into either *original* equation.
- Solve the resulting equation.
- Check by substituting both values into *all original equations*.

  **MODEL PROBLEMS**

1. Solve the system of equations $x + y = 8$ and $x - y = 2$.

Solution:
The equations are already in standard form, and the y terms are already opposites.

$x + y = 8$ Set up the equations in columns.

$\underline{x - y = 2}$

$2x = 10$ Add the columns.

$\dfrac{2x}{2} = \dfrac{10}{2}$ Solve for x.

$x = 5$

$(5) + y = 8$ Substitute 5 for x the first equation

$\underline{{}^{-}5 \quad\quad = {}^{-}5}$

$y = 3$ Solve for y.

Check. Substitute 5 for x and 3 for y in the original equations.

$$x + y = 8$$
$$(5) + (3) = 8$$
$$8 = 8 \checkmark$$

$$x - y = 2$$
$$(5) - (3) = 2$$
$$2 = 2 \checkmark$$

Answer: $(5, 3)$

2. Find the solution of the system $x - 2y = 1$ and $x + y = 10$.

Solution:

	The coefficients of x are the same.
$x - 2y = 1$	Write the first equation.
$(^-1)x + (^-1)(^-2y) = (^-1)1$	Multiply each term by $^-1$.
$-x + 2y = {}^-1$	Simplify.
$\underline{x + y = 10}$	Set up the equations in columns and add.
$3y = 9$	
$y = 3$	Solve.
$x + y = 10$	Replace x in either equation.
$x + 3 = 10$	
$x = 7$	

Check by substituting 3 for y and 7 for x in both original equations.

$$x - 2y = 1$$
$$7 - 2(3) = 1$$
$$7 - 6 = 1 \checkmark$$

$$x + y = 10$$
$$7 + 3 = 10 \checkmark$$

Answer: $(7, 3)$

3. Solve the system $5x - 2y = 10$ and $2x + y = 31$.

Solution:

	More work is involved to make the y coefficients cancel.
$2x + y = 31$	Write the second equation.
$(2)2x + (2)y = (2)31$	Multiply each term by 2.
$4x + 2y = 62$	Simplify.
$5x - 2y = 10$	Set up the equations in columns and add.
$\underline{4x + 2y = 62}$	

$$9x = 72$$
$$x = 8$$
$$2x + y = 31$$
$$2(8) + y = 31$$
$$16 + y = 31$$
$$y = 15$$

Solve.

Replace x in either equation.

Check by substituting 15 for y and 8 for x in both original equations.

$$5x - 2y \qquad = 10$$
$$5(8) - 2(15) = 10$$
$$40 - 30 \qquad = 10 \checkmark$$

$$2x + y \qquad = 31$$
$$2(8) + (15) = 31$$
$$16 + 15 = 31 \checkmark$$

Answer: (8, 15)

To Solve Systems of Equations with the Substitution Method

- Solve one of the equations for one of the variables.
- Substitute the resulting algebraic expression in the second equation.
- Solve the second equation for the second variable.
- Substitute the resulting value in either original equation.
- Solve for the first variable.
- Check by substituting both values in the equation no used in step 4.

 # MODEL PROBLEMS

1. Solve this system of equations: $3x - 4y = 2$ and $x = 14 - 2y$.

Solution:

Since the solutions are the same for each equation, $x = 14 - 2y$ is true in both equations.

$$3x - 4y = 2$$ Write the first equation.

$$3(14 - 2y) - 4y = 2$$ Substitute $14 - 2y$ for x.

$$42 - 6y - 4y = 2$$ Distribute the 3.

$$42 - 10y = 2$$ Combine like terms.

$$42 = 10y + 2$$ Add $10y$ to both sides.

$$40 = 10y$$ Subtract 2 from both sides.

$$4 = y$$ Solve.

Substitute 4 for y in either equation.

$x = 14 - 2y$

$x = 14 - 2(4)$

$x = 14 - 8 = 6$

Check by substituting 6 for x and 4 for y in both original equations.

$3x - 4y = 2$ $x = 14 - 2y$

$3(6) - 4(4) = 2$ $6 = 14 - 2(4)$

$18 - 16 = 2$ ✓ $6 = 14 - 8$ ✓

Answer: $(6, 4)$

2. Henrietta has seven bills, all tens and twenties, that total \$100 in value. How many of each bill does she have?

Solution:

Let x represent the number of tens and y represent the number of twenties.

Henrietta's number of bills can be shown by $x + y = 7$.

The cash value of the bills can be shown by $10x + 20y = 100$.

Now we have the systems $x + y = 7$ and $10x + 2y = 100$.

$x + y = 7$	Write the first equation.
$\underline{-y = -y}$	Solve for x.
$x \quad\;\; = 7 - y$	
$10x + 20y = 100$	Write the second equation.
$10(7 - y) + 20y = 100$	Substitute $(7 - y)$ for x.
$70 - 10y + 20y = 100$	Solve.
$70 \qquad + 10y = 100$	
$\underline{^-70 \qquad\qquad\quad = {}^-70}$	
$10y = 30$	
$y = 3$	

Substitute 3 for y in one of the original equations and solve for x.

$x + y = 7$

$x + (3) = 7$

$\underline{\quad\quad {}^-3 = {}^-3}$

$x = 4$

To check, substitute 3 for y and 4 for x in each equation.

$10x + 20y = 100$ $x + y = 7$

$10(4) + 20(3) = 100$ $3 + 4 = 7$ ✓

$40 + 60 = 100$ ✓

Check the original problem.

4 bills + 3 bills = 7 bills

$(4 \times 10) + (3 \times 20) = 40 + 60 = 100$

Answer: Henrietta has 4 ten-dollar bills and 3 twenty-dollar bills.

1. You want to solve the system below by eliminating y. You multiply the first equation by 7. By what number should you multiply the second equation?

$2x - 5y = 1$
$^-3x + 7y = ^-3$

A $^-7$
B $^-5$
C 5
D 7

2. What is the solution to this system of equations?

$2x + y = 7$
$3x - y = 3$

F $(4, 1)$
G $(2, ^-1)$
H $(2, 3)$
J $(3, 2)$

3. Prestige Parking charges $5 for the first hour or any part of that hour and $3 per hour for each additional hour or part of an hour. Paradise Parking charges $8 for the first hour or any part of that hour and $1.50 per hour for each additional hour or part of an hour. For how many hours of parking will the charge be the same in both garages?

A From 1 hour and 1 minute to 2 hours
B From 2 hours and 1 minute to 3 hours
C From 3 hours and 1 minute to 4 hours
D From 4 hours and 1 minute to 5 hours

4. A circus act has 3 times as many elephants as acrobats. Jorge noticed that all together, there were 56 legs in the circus ring. How many elephants were in the show?

F 14 elephants
G 12 elephants
H 9 elephants
J 4 elephants

5. What is the solution to this system of equations?

$2x + y = 12$
$x + 2y = 9$

6. In the vote for school president, 476 seniors voted for one or the other of the two candidates. The candidate who won had a majority of 94. How many seniors were for the winner?

7. The sum of two numbers is 78. Their difference is 18. Find the numbers.

8. The factory foreman makes $9 more per hour than Janet, the most senior worker. If one dollar is subtracted from the foreman's rate of pay, the resulting amount is $\frac{3}{2}$ what Janet makes. Find the rate of pay for Janet and the foreman.

9. Carlos and Sam together unpacked cartons for 3 hours at a rate of 8 cartons per hour. During that time, Carlos unpacked twice as many cartons as Sam. How many cartons did each of them unpack?

10. Justin ordered a hamburger and soda. His cost was $4.75. Anthony ordered two hamburgers. His cost was $5.50. What was the cost of the soda?

To Solve Systems of Equations Graphically

- Draw the graph of each equation on the same coordinate plane.
- The coordinates of the point of intersection of the graphs are the required values of x and y.
- Check the solution in both original equations.

 MODEL PROBLEM

The perimeter of a rectangular vegetable patch is 12 feet and the length is twice the width. Find the dimensions of the vegetable patch by setting up a system of equations and solving graphically.

Solution:

Let x represent the width and y represent the length.

We know that $2x + 2y = 12$, or $x + y = 6$.

We also know that $y = 2x$.

Therefore, the two equations for this system are $x + y = 6$ and $y = 2x$.

Graph the two equations on the same coordinate plane and label the point of intersection.

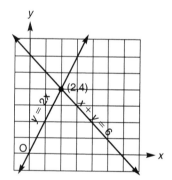

Check the solution (2, 4) in both original equations:

$x + y = 6$	$y = 2x$
$2 + 4 = 6$	$4 = 2(2)$
$6 = 6$ ✓	$4 = 4$ ✓

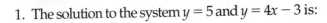

PRACTICE

1. The solution to the system $y = 5$ and $y = 4x - 3$ is:

   A $(5, 17)$
   B $(2, 5)$
   C $(0, 5)$
   D No solution

2. The lines $y = 2x + 2$ and $y = 3x - 1$ intersect at point:

   F $(^-3, ^-8)$
   G $(^-1, ^-4)$
   H $(1, 4)$
   J $(3, 8)$

   For problems 3 through 10, solve each system of equations graphically and check.

3. $x + y = 4$
   $\quad y = 3x$

4. $y = ^-x + 7$
   $\quad y = 2x + 1$

5. $x - y = 4$
   $\quad y = \dfrac{1}{2}x$

6. $2x + y = 2$
   $\quad y - x = 5$

7. $y - x = 2$
   $\quad y - 2x - 2 = 0$

8. $x = 0$
   $\quad y = ^-3$

9. $y = ^-3x$
   $\quad 2x + y + 2 = 0$

10. $y = ^-2x - 1$
    $\quad x + y + 4 = 0$

4.9 LINEAR INEQUALITIES

A line graphed in the coordinate plane divides the plane into two regions, called *half-planes*. When the equation of the line is written in slope-intercept form or $y = mx + b$ form, the half-plane *above* the line is the graph of $y > mx + b$ and the half-plane *below* the line is the graph of $y < mx + b$. If a half-plane is to be included in a solution set, we show this by shading its entire region. The line itself, considered a *boundary line*, is drawn as a solid line when it is part of the solution set and as a dashed line if it is not.

To Graph a Linear Inequality

- Graph the boundary line for the inequality by expressing the inequality as an equation in slope-intercept form or by creating a table of values.

   If the sign is $>$ or $<$, the boundary line will be broken or dashed.
   If the sign is $\geq$ or $\leq$, the boundary line will be solid.

- Shade the half-plane of the inequality.

   Method 1: Select two points, one on each side of the boundary line, and substitute them into the inequality. Shade the half-plane with the point that makes the inequality true.

   Method 2: Solve the inequality for y or for x.

   If the inequality begins with $y >$ or $y \geq$, shade the half-plane *above* the boundary line. If the inequality begins with $y <$ or $y \leq$, shade the half-plane *below* the boundary line.

   If the inequality begins with $x >$ or $x \geq$, shade the half-plane to the *right* of the boundary line.

   If the inequality begins with $x <$ or $x \leq$, shade the half-plane to the *left* of the boundary line.

 MODEL PROBLEMS

1. Graph $y > 2x + 1$ and $y < 2x + 1$

Solution:

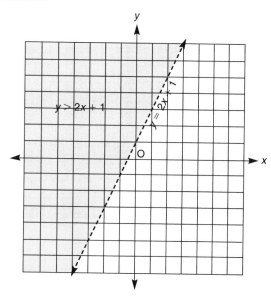

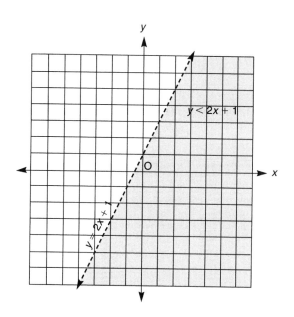

2. Graph $y \geq 2x + 1$ and check.

Solution:

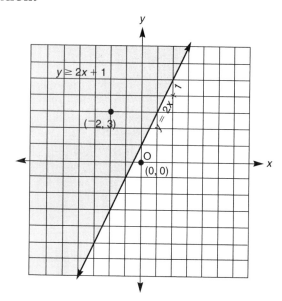

Check (⁻2, 3) by substituting.

$$y \geq 2x + 1$$
$$3 \geq 2(⁻2) + 1$$
$$3 \geq ⁻4 + 1$$
$$3 \geq ⁻3 ✓$$

Check (0, 0) from outside the solution set.

$$y \geq 2x + 1$$
$$0 \geq 2(0) + 1$$
$$0 \geq 0 + 1$$
$$0 \ngeq 1 \text{ (not in solution set) } ✓$$

3. Graph the inequality $x - 3y > 6$.

Solution:

Rewrite the inequality in $y = mx + b$ form:

$$x - 3y > 6$$
$$x - 6 > 3y \text{ or } 3y < x - 6$$
$$y < \frac{x}{3} - 2$$

Create a table of values for $y = \dfrac{x}{3} - 2$.

x	⁻3	0	3
y	⁻3	⁻2	⁻1

Graph the inequality.

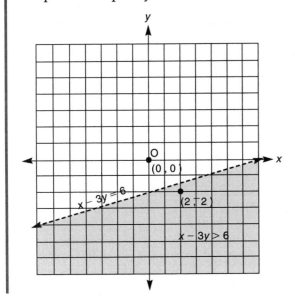

Check (2, ⁻2) by substituting

$$x - 3y > 6$$
$$(2) - 3(^-2) > 6$$
$$2 + 6 > 6$$
$$8 > 6 ✓$$

Check (0, 0) from outside the solution set.

$$x - 3y > 6$$
$$(0) - 3(0) > 6$$
$$0 \not> 6 \text{ (not in solution set) } ✓$$

4. Graph $x > 3$ and $x \leq 3$ on separate coordinate planes.

Solution:

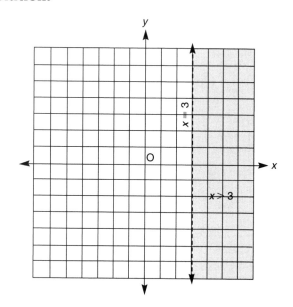 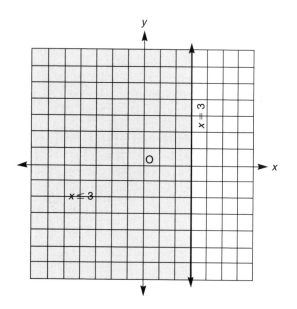

1. Which graph shows $y < 3x$?

A

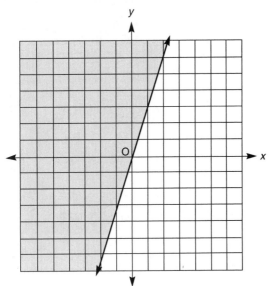

C

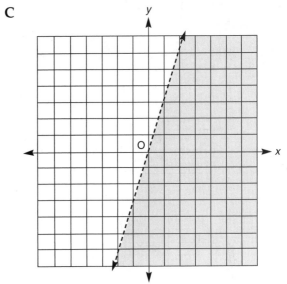

B

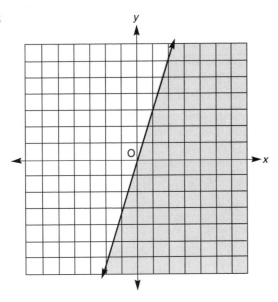

D

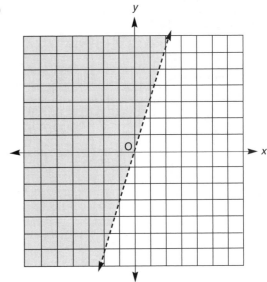

2. Which graph shows $y > ^-x - 1$?

F

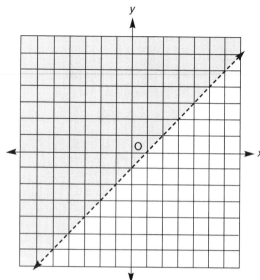

H

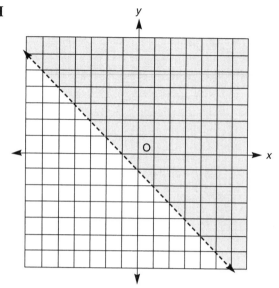

G

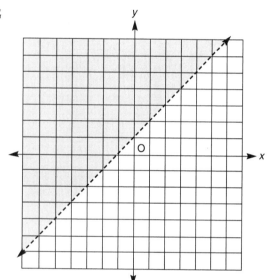

J

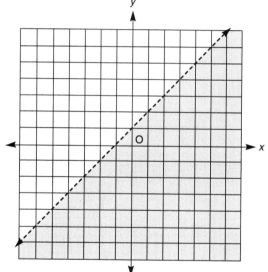

3. Which inequality best describes the graph shown below?

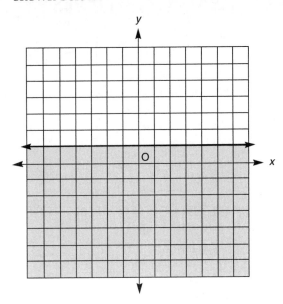

A $y > 1$
B $y < 1$
C $y \le 1$
D $y \ge 1$

4. Which inequality best describes the graph shown below?

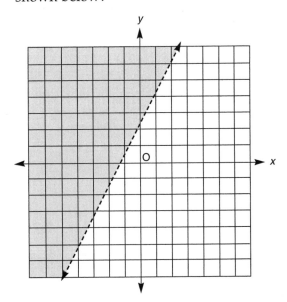

F $y \le \frac{1}{2}x + 2$

G $y \ge -\frac{1}{2}x + 2$

H $y < {}^-2x + 2$

J $y > 2x + 2$

For problems 5 through 10, graph each inequality.

5. $y \le {}^-2x$

6. $x + y \ge 1$

7. $2x + y > {}^-4$

8. $2x - y < 3$

9. $x \le 0$

10. $x < 1 + y + x$

Graphs are used to represent relationships between two variables. They help us understand the relationships and often help us generalize beyond the data supplied. In functions, a value of y is assigned to each value of x. The primary relationship in a function is that the y-value depends on the x-value. For this reason, the x-axis is called the *independent axis* and the y-axis is called the *dependent axis*.

Drawing the Graph of a Situation

In dealing with real situations, it becomes necessary to think of the x-axis as some independent variable, such as time, and to think of the y-axis as a dependent variable, such as height or distance. Whenever it is clear that one variable depends on the other, the dependent variable should be the y and the independent variable should be the x. If a graph is comparing air pressure at different altitudes, then the pressure, y, depends on the altitude, x. But if a graph is charting a mountain climber's progress, the altitude, y, depends on the time spent climbing, x.

MODEL PROBLEM

Deluxe Limousine Service charges $2 for the initial pickup of a passenger and then $1 per mile. Make a graph of this situation.

Solution:

Note that the fee for the ride *depends* upon the number miles traveled. Therefore, the fee will be represented by the variable y and distance will be represented by the variable x. The equation will then be $y = \$2 + \$1x$.

We can make a table of miles and fees for Deluxe Limousine Service. The label for the x-axis is *miles traveled* and the label for the y-axis is *taxi fee in dollars*.

Miles Traveled x	Taxi Fee in Dollars y
0	2
1	3
2	4

The graph starts where the number of miles traveled is 0. The fee at zero miles is $2. Thus the point $(0, 2)$ is on the graph. A 1-mile trip costs $3 and 2-mile trip costs $4. When we plot these points, we see a linear pattern. We can extend the graph in the first quadrant and we can read the fees for longer trips.

Answer:

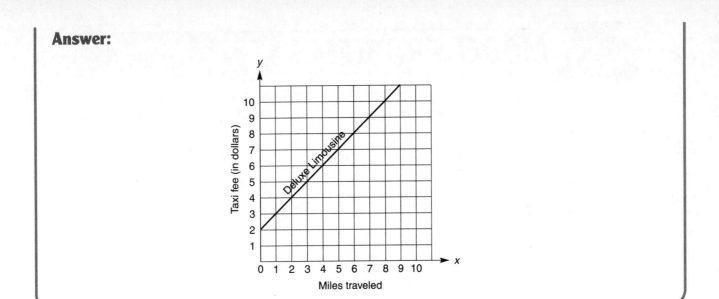

Reading the Graph of a Situation

Sometimes we are given the graph of a situation and then asked various questions about the situation. When answering these questions, remember the following:

- Questions that involve rates (time per room painted, daily charge) or speeds (miles per hour, births per year) will usually require information about the slope.
- Questions that involve starting times, opening saving accounts, beginning locations, or similar *initial conditions* are usually asking questions about the *y*-intercept.
- Questions that start "When will…" or "How many…" usually provide a value for one variable and expect you to find the value for the other variable from the corresponding point on the graph.

This graph represents the billing structure for Friendly Taxi. What is the initial pickup fee and charge per mile for this service?

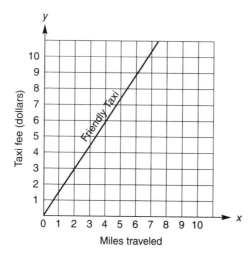

Solution:

The initial picked up fee is the charge before any driving is done, in other words when x is 0. The point on the graph with an x value of zero is the origin, $(0, 0)$. Therefore, the pickup fee is $0.

The charge per mile is the change in price per change in miles, or $\frac{\Delta y}{\Delta x}$, the slope. Two points on the line include $(0, 0)$ and $(2, 3)$, so $\frac{\Delta y}{\Delta x} = \frac{3 - 0}{2 - 0} = \frac{3 \text{ dollars}}{2 \text{ miles}} = 1.5$ dollars per mile.

Answer: There is no pickup fee, and the charge per mile is $1.50.

Nonlinear Functions as Graphs of Situations

Nonlinear graphs appear often in real situations. Answering questions about non-linear functions is similar to answering questions about linear functions. Remember:

- Questions that start with "When will…" and "How many…" usually provide a value for one variable and expect you find the value for the other variable from the corresponding point on the graph.

Situations Involving Graphs of Systems

When two equations are graphed on the same coordinate plane, many types of questions involve comparing the graphs.

- Questions that ask "When is situation A better/lower than situation B?" want you to find an inequality involving x that describes what part of the graph satisfies the situation. For example, the answer might be "When the time is longer than 5 days."
- Questions that ask "When are the values the same?" want you to find the coordinates of the point of intersection.
- Questions that ask about differences at specific values of x require you to subtract the y-value of one line from the other.

Deluxe Limousine Service charges $2 for the initial pickup of a passenger and then $1 per mile. By comparison, Friendly Taxi does not have an initial pickup charge but charges $1.50 per mile. Graph the fee schedule for Deluxe Limousine on the same coordinate plane as the graph for Friendly Taxi. Then answer the following questions:
- For what length trips is it cheaper to use Friendly Taxi?
- At what mileage is the cost the same for both services? What is the cost?
- What is the difference in cost at the 6-mile mark?

Solution:

The graphs of the costs of each service were discussed earlier in this section. By graphing them on the same coordinate plane, you can answer the three questions.

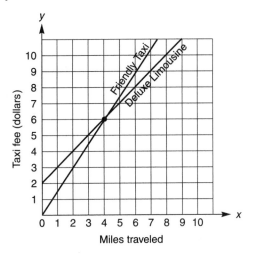

Answers:

- The graph for Friendly Taxi is below the graph for Deluxe Limousine up to the 4-mile mark. So for trips under 4 miles long, it is cheaper to use Friendly Taxi.
- The lines intersect at (4, 6). So at 4 miles, the cost for both services is $6.
- At 6 miles, the graph shows the cost for Deluxe Limousine is $8 and the cost for Friendly Taxi is $9. The difference is $9 − $8 = $1.

PRACTICE

1. Terry and Claire had a list of eight books they each had to read over the summer. They decided to race each other to see who would finish first. According to the results in the figure, who reads faster and by how much?

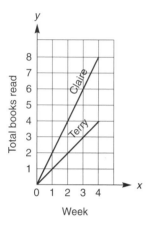

A Claire reads 8 books more per week than Terry.

B Claire reads 2 books more per week than Terry.

C Claire reads 1 book more per week than Terry.

D Claire reads twice as many books per weeks as Terry.

2. Alyssa bicycled for 2 hours at 4 miles per hour. She stopped for one hour to visit a friend. She bicycled for another hour at 5 miles per hour. Which graph best represents Alyssa's trip if the horizontal axis is time and the vertical axis is distance?

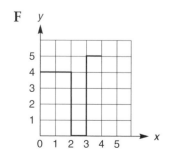

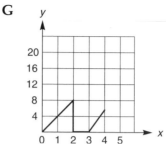

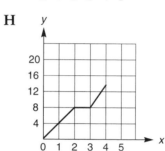

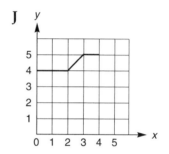

3. The profit that a bookstore makes is related to the number of books purchased, as shown in the graph below.

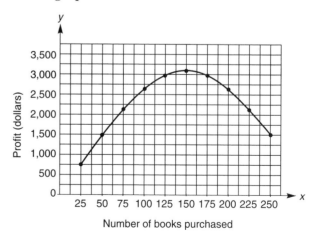

How many books must be purchased for the bookstore to make the maximum profit?

A 100 **C** 200

B 150 **D** 250

144 Chapter 4: Patterns and Functions

4. The graph below shows the time of sunset in Baltimore for the months of January to December.

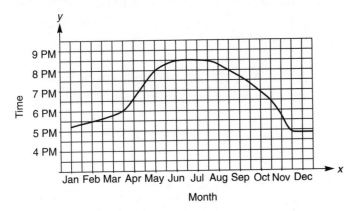

During which of these months did the sunset the earliest?

F January

G April

H July

J November

5. Both Janine and Fran used exercise equipment at their gym. Fran walked on a treadmill and Janine rode a stationary bicycle. Their times and calories burned are shown in the graph below. In calories burned per hour, how much faster was Janine than Fran?

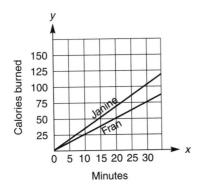

6. The accompanying graph shows the closing price per share of a certain stock over a period of 7 days. (Note that a price such as $1\frac{1}{2}$ dollars is $1.50)

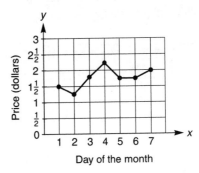

Between what two days did the price decrease most sharply? How much did the price decrease over those two days?

7. The graph below shows the cost of membership for two recreational clubs. For each club, the cost includes an initial fee to join the club plus a monthly charge.

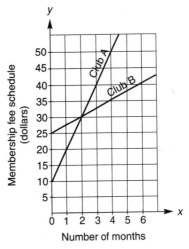

Answer the following:

- What is the initial fee for Club A? For Club B?
- For which month will the total expenses be the same for both clubs? What is the total cost?
- What is the monthly charge for Club A? For Club B?

8. Two different health clubs have the following rates. Sammi's Spa charges a flat fee of $350 a year for the use of the club, machines, the pool, and the classes. Shape Up! charges $150 a year for the use of the club, machines, and pool, plus $20 per exercise class.

- Write an equation to represent each health club's yearly fees.
- Graph each equation with appropriate labels for the axes.
- Under what circumstances is it more economical to join Shape Up!

Assessment　Chapter 4

1. Which of the following is NOT a geometric sequence?

   A 1, 1, 1, 1, 1, . . .
   B 10, 100, 1,000, 10,000, . . .
   C 6, 4, 2, 0, ⁻2, . . .
   D 6, 3, 1.5, 0.75, . . .

2. Which of the following diagrams does NOT represent a function?

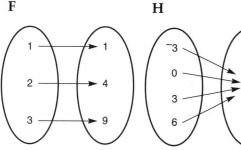

3. What digit is in the 20th decimal place in the decimal value of $\frac{35}{101}$?

   A 3　　**B** 4　　**C** 5　　**D** 6

4. What is the units digit in 12^{15}?

   F 2　　**G** 4　　**H** 6　　**J** 8

5. Given the pattern TEXASTEXASTEXAS . . . , what letter is in the 99th position?

   A A　　**B** T　　**C** X　　**D** S

6. Which graph corresponds to $x - y = 5$?

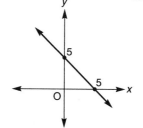
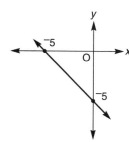
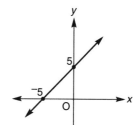
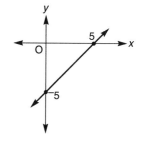
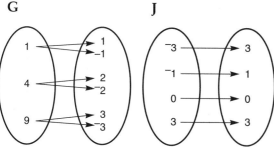

7. The table illustrates the function $y = {}^-2x - 2$. What value do you get for y when $x = {}^-6$?

x	y
0	${}^-2$
1	${}^-4$
2	${}^-6$

A 14 **B** 10 **C** ${}^-10$ **D** ${}^-14$

8. Solve the following system of equations. $x + 2y = 10$ and $3x - 2y = 6$

F $(4, 2)$ **H** $(1, {}^-4.5)$
G $(4, 3)$ **J** $(1, 4.5)$

9. A sequence is generated by the rule $3n^2 - 4$, where n represents the number of the term in the sequence. What is the difference in the values of the 25th and 26th terms in the sequence?

A 6 **B** 153 **C** 159 **D** 459

10. In January, a certain item sells for $10.00. In February, the price increases 10%. In March, it decreases 10%. In April, it increases 10%, and so on. (It continues to alternate between the 10% increase and 10% decrease.) Which of the following graphs is suggested by the situation described above?

F

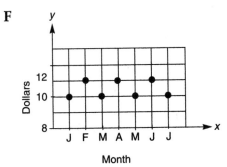

G

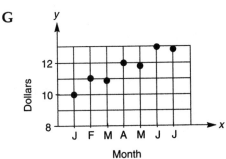

H

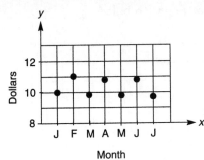

J

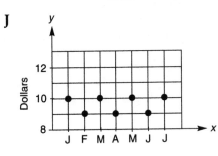

11. A function uses the following rules:

a. Input any number greater than or equal to zero, and the function yields the same value that was input.

b. Input any negative number, and the function yields the opposite of that number.

Which of the following graphs matches the description of the function?

A

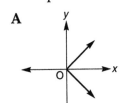

C

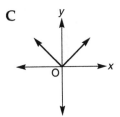

B

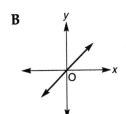

D

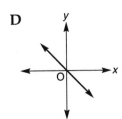

12. Look at the graph below.

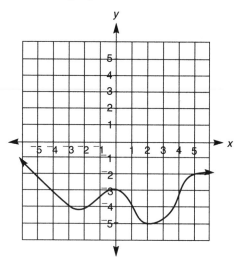

There is a minimum at

F $x = 2$ H $y = 2$

G $x = 5$ J $y = 5$

13. If the horizontal axis is used for time and the vertical axis is used for price, which graph shows the sharpest increase in price over a period of time?

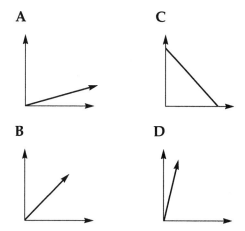

A   C

B   D

14. What is the difference between the 15th terms of sequence A and sequence B?

sequence A: 2, 4, 8, 16, . . .
sequence B: ⁻2, 4, ⁻8, 16, . . .

F 0   H 32,768
G 16,384   J 65,536

15. The number of mold cells on a piece of bread doubles every 12 minutes. If there are 35 mold cells on the bread now, about how many cells will there be 2 hours from now?

A 420   B 840   C 2,458   D 35,840

16. Suppose you start with $39.65 in your bank. Each day you put in $1.35 more than you put in on the previous day. That is, on day 1 you put in $1.35, on day 2 you put in $1.35 + $1.35 or $2.70, on day 3, $4.05, and so on. How much money will you have in the bank on the 12th day?

F $55.85   H $144.95
G $128.75   J $492

17. At We-Carry, shipping charges are $4.25 for the first 3 pounds and 75¢ for each additional pound. At that rate, how much did a package weigh if the charges were $11?

A 6 pounds   C 12 pounds
B 9 pounds   D 15 pounds

18. Which of the following lines has a negative slope?

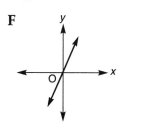

F   H

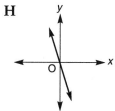

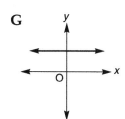

G   J

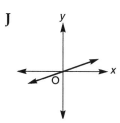

19. Which of the following points is NOT on the graph of $3x + y = 15$?

A (5, 0)   B (⁻5, 0)   C (3, 6)   D (6, ⁻3)

20. Which of the following equations represents the line containing the points given in the graph?

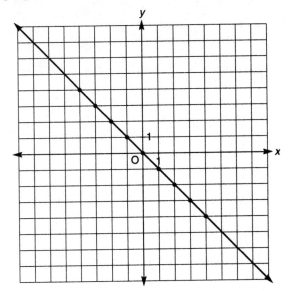

F $y = x$ **H** $x - y = 0$
G $y + x = 0$ **J** $y = x - 1$

21. Study the graph below.

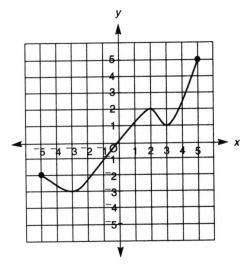

What is the range of the function?

A $^-5 \leq x \leq 2$
B $^-3 \leq x \leq 5$
C $^-5 \leq y \leq 2$
D $^-3 \leq y \leq 5$

22. Look at the graph below.

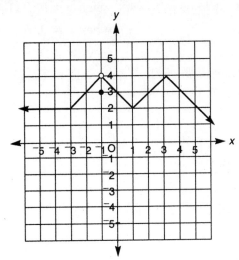

The function is not continuous at

F $(^-2, 3)$
G $(^-1, 4)$
H $(3, 5)$
J $(5, 3)$

23. What is the slope of the line that passes through the points $(4, 2)$ and $(^-9, 3)$?

A $^-13$

B $-\dfrac{1}{13}$

C $\dfrac{1}{13}$

D 13

24. What is the range of the function $f(x) = -\dfrac{1}{4}x^2 - 6$ when the domain is $\{^-2, ^-1, 4, 8\}$?

F $\{^-5, ^-2, ^-7, ^-10\}$
G $\{^-7, 10, 20, 22\}$
H $\{^-7, ^-6.5, ^-10, ^-22\}$
J $\{2, ^-10, 5, 10\}$

25. A function is defined for the domain of all real numbers as follows: when $x < 0$, $f(x) = 6$

    when $x = 0$, $f(x) = 0$

    when $x > 0$, $f(x) = {}^-6$

Which of the following would be the graph of the function described?

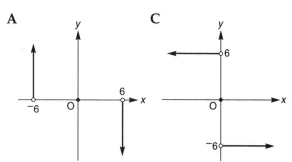

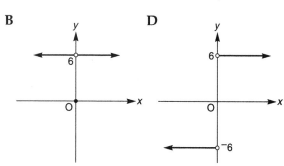

26. Which of the following equations is TRUE for all values that could replace x?

  F $3(x - 2) = 3x - 6$

  G $15 - x = x - 15$

  H $\dfrac{x}{6} = \dfrac{6}{x}$

  J $7(x - 5) = 7x - 5$

27. Note the following pattern:

  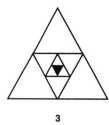

    1   2   3

If the pattern is extended, what percent of the 5th diagram would be shaded?

  A Less than 1%   **C** 40%

  B 4%   **D** 400%

28. Find the sum of the infinite geometric series

$$1 + \frac{1}{3} + \frac{1}{9} + \frac{1}{27} + \ldots$$

  F $\dfrac{1}{3}$ **G** $\dfrac{2}{3}$ **H** $\dfrac{3}{2}$ **J** 3

29. For the arithmetic series $1 + 4 + 7 + 10 + \ldots + 97 + 100$ the sum is:

  A 150   **B** 606   **C** 1,700   **D** 1,717

30. If $y = f(x) = x^3$, which of the following is NOT true?

  F $f(x)$ is a function.

  G $\left| f({}^-4) \right| = \left| f(4) \right|$

  H $f(x)$ is a periodic function.

  J $f(x)$ does not have a constant slope.

31. This graph shows the cost of electricity:

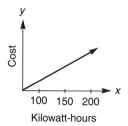

Which of the following statements is not true concerning this graph?

  A The graph illustrates a function.

  B The graph shows that the cost of electricity levels off at some point.

  C As the number of kilowatt-hours increases, the cost also increases.

  D The cost increases at the same rate between 100–500 kilowatts-hours and 150–200 kilowatt-hours.

32. Evaluate $a^b + b^a$ when $a = 5$ and $b = 2$.

33. What is the equation of a line containing the point $(3, 3)$ if the line is parallel to a line passing through the points $({}^-2, 0)$ and $(0, 8)$?

34. Here is a function represented in words:

   The cost of mailing a first class letter depends on the weight of the letter.

   - What is the independent variable?
   - What is the dependent variable?
   - State two other ways to represent this function.

35. Consider the following pattern:

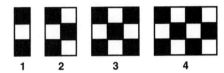

   If the pattern is continued, how many small squares would be shaded in the 9th diagram?

36. A special sequence is formed by taking 5 more than the sum of the two previous terms to find the third term and all succeeding terms. If the first four terms of the sequence are 1, 2, 8, 15, . . . , find the 10th term.

37. The first four terms of an arithmetic sequence are 3, 7, 11, 15, and 123 is the 31st term. What is the value of the 30th term?

38. - Plot the ordered pairs (8, 0), (7, 1), (6, 2), (5, 3).
   - Sketch the graph suggested by the ordered pairs.
   - Describe the pattern in words.
   - What equation describes the pattern?

Extended Constructed Response Questions

39. Starlite Pizzeria has regular expenses of $500 per week. In addition, their cost is $3 on average for each pizza made. They charge $8 for a pizza (this is the average price regardless of topping).

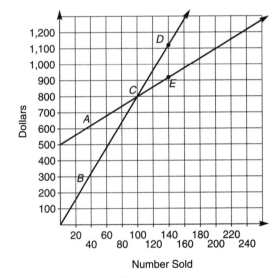

Using the given graph:

- Identify the line that represents expenses and the line that represents revenue (income).
- Explain the significance of point C.
- What is the significance of the value of D less the value of E?

40. Miguel has read five novels this summer. His goal is to read two more by the end of each month.

   - Write an equation in slope-intercept form to represent the situation.
   - Draw the graph that illustrates the relationship.
   - If Miguel continues this process, how many novels will he have read at the end of two years? Show your work.

41. Consider the pattern shown.

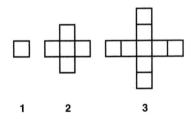

   - If the pattern is extended, how many small squares would there be in the 20th picture?
   - Explain why the number of small squares would always be 1 more than a multiple of 4.

42. Alexandra purchases two doughnuts and three cookies at a doughnut shop and is charged $3.30. Briana purchases five doughnuts and two cookies at the same shop for $4.95. All the doughnuts have the same price and all the cookies have the same price. Find the cost of one doughnut and find the cost of one cookie.

43. Draw a graph representing a function that satisfies all the following clues:

    I. The domain is $^-4 \leq x \leq 4$

    II. The range is $1 \leq y \leq 5$

    III. $f(^-4) = f(^-2) = f(0) = f(2) = f(4) = 1$

    IV. $f(^-3) = f(^-1) = f(1) = f(3) = 5$

Answer Document

Sample HSA Test _____

Name: _____

Session 1

1. Ⓐ Ⓑ Ⓒ Ⓓ

2. Ⓕ Ⓖ Ⓗ Ⓙ

3. Ⓐ Ⓑ Ⓒ Ⓓ

4. Ⓕ Ⓖ Ⓗ Ⓙ

5. Ⓐ Ⓑ Ⓒ Ⓓ

6. Use the space provided below.

7. Ⓕ Ⓖ Ⓗ Ⓙ

8. Ⓐ Ⓑ Ⓒ Ⓓ

9. Ⓕ Ⓖ Ⓗ Ⓙ

10. Ⓐ Ⓑ Ⓒ Ⓓ

11. Ⓕ Ⓖ Ⓗ Ⓙ

12. Use the space provided below.

13.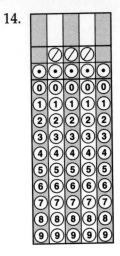

/	/	/
·	·	·	·	·
0	0	0	0	0
1	1	1	1	1
2	2	2	2	2
3	3	3	3	3
4	4	4	4	4
5	5	5	5	5
6	6	6	6	6
7	7	7	7	7
8	8	8	8	8
9	9	9	9	9

14.

/	/	/
·	·	·	·	·
0	0	0	0	0
1	1	1	1	1
2	2	2	2	2
3	3	3	3	3
4	4	4	4	4
5	5	5	5	5
6	6	6	6	6
7	7	7	7	7
8	8	8	8	8
9	9	9	9	9

15.

/	/	/
·	·	·	·	·
0	0	0	0	0
1	1	1	1	1
2	2	2	2	2
3	3	3	3	3
4	4	4	4	4
5	5	5	5	5
6	6	6	6	6
7	7	7	7	7
8	8	8	8	8
9	9	9	9	9

16. Use the space provided below.

17. Ⓐ Ⓑ Ⓒ Ⓓ

18. Ⓕ Ⓖ Ⓗ Ⓙ

19. Ⓐ Ⓑ Ⓒ Ⓓ

20. Ⓕ Ⓖ Ⓗ Ⓙ

21. Use the space provided below.

22. Ⓐ Ⓑ Ⓒ Ⓓ

23. Ⓕ Ⓖ Ⓗ Ⓙ

24. Ⓐ Ⓑ Ⓒ Ⓓ

25. Ⓕ Ⓖ Ⓗ Ⓙ

26. (A)(B)(C)(D)

27. (F)(G)(H)(J)

28. (A)(B)(C)(D)

29. (F)(G)(H)(J)

30. Use the space provided below.

31. Ⓐ Ⓑ Ⓒ Ⓓ

32. Ⓕ Ⓖ Ⓗ Ⓙ

33. Ⓐ Ⓑ Ⓒ Ⓓ

34. Ⓕ Ⓖ Ⓗ Ⓙ

35. Use the space provided below.

36.

	⊘	⊘	⊘	
•	•	•	•	•
⓪	⓪	⓪	⓪	⓪
①	①	①	①	①
②	②	②	②	②
③	③	③	③	③
④	④	④	④	④
⑤	⑤	⑤	⑤	⑤
⑥	⑥	⑥	⑥	⑥
⑦	⑦	⑦	⑦	⑦
⑧	⑧	⑧	⑧	⑧
⑨	⑨	⑨	⑨	⑨

37.

	⊘	⊘		
•	•	•	•	•
⓪	⓪	⓪	⓪	⓪
①	①	①	①	①
②	②	②	②	②
③	③	③	③	③
④	④	④	④	④
⑤	⑤	⑤	⑤	⑤
⑥	⑥	⑥	⑥	⑥
⑦	⑦	⑦	⑦	⑦
⑧	⑧	⑧	⑧	⑧
⑨	⑨	⑨	⑨	⑨

38.

	⊘	⊘		
•	•	•	•	•
⓪	⓪	⓪	⓪	⓪
①	①	①	①	①
②	②	②	②	②
③	③	③	③	③
④	④	④	④	④
⑤	⑤	⑤	⑤	⑤
⑥	⑥	⑥	⑥	⑥
⑦	⑦	⑦	⑦	⑦
⑧	⑧	⑧	⑧	⑧
⑨	⑨	⑨	⑨	⑨

39. Ⓐ Ⓑ Ⓒ Ⓓ

40. Ⓕ Ⓖ Ⓗ Ⓙ

41. Ⓐ Ⓑ Ⓒ Ⓓ

42. Ⓕ Ⓖ Ⓗ Ⓙ

Session 1

1. The price of drinks at the Green Deli is shown in the matrix below. Fivebucks charges three times the price of drinks at the Green Deli.

$$\begin{array}{c} \\ \text{Soda} \\ \text{Tea} \end{array} \begin{array}{ccc} \text{S} & \text{M} & \text{L} \\ \left[\begin{array}{ccc} 1.00 & 1.25 & 1.75 \\ 0.75 & 1.00 & 1.50 \end{array}\right] \end{array}$$

Daniel bought two medium teas and one large soda from Fivebucks, how much did he pay altogether?

A $3.75
B $4.25
C $10.50
D $11.25

2. Look at the graph of the function below.

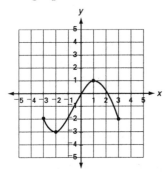

What is the domain of this function?

F $^-5 \le x \le 5$
G $^-5 \le x \le 3$
H $^-3 \le x \le 3$
J $^-2 \le x \le 3$

3. Tony travels at a constant speed during a road trip. After 4 hours, he stops for an hour to eat and rest. Then he continues for 5 more hours at the same speed.

Which of the following graphs best represents this situation?

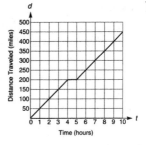

4. In order to pay for expenses, a week long summer camp needs at least $86,000. The camp receives $300 per person for half-day campers and $450 for full-day campers. Which of these combinations would be enough to pay for expenses?

F 74 half-day and 176 full-day campers
G 176 half-day and 74 full-day campers
H 70 half-day and 50 full-day campers
J 50 half-day and 100 full-day campers

5. Which statements are true?

I. The interquartile range is half the distance between the lower quartile and the upper quartile.
II. The interquartile range is not affected by outliers.
III. The median represents the 50th percentile.

A I and II
B II only
C II and III
D I and III

Question 6 is a Brief Constructed Response Item.

6. The annual salaries for five major-league baseball players are:

$120,000 $110,000 $140,000
$120,000 $1,000,000

- Find the mean for the salaries.
- What is the median salary?
- Which of the two measures (mean or median) gives a better indication of the annual salary for the group of baseball players? Explain your response.

7. Tanya saved $300 to spend on her vacation. She must have $70 left to pay for her airplane ticket home and she plans on spending about $40 per day. Which of the following inequalities best represents the possible numbers of days Tanya could be on vacation?

F $300 − $40d ≥ $70
G $300 − $40d ≤ $70
H $300 − $70d ≥ $40
J $300 − $70d ≤ $40

8. Ellen is x years old. Justina is three years older than Ellen. Ellen's mother is 10 years older than twice Ellen's current age. Which of the following expressions represents how much older is Ellen's mother is than Justina?

A 2x + 10
B (2x + 10) − x
C (2x + 10) − (x + 3)
D 3x − x

9. How many solutions does the following system of equations have?

3y + 6x = 15
y = ⁻2x + 5

F Infinite solutions
G No solutions
H One solution
J Two solutions

10. A bag contains 3 round blue pegs, 2 round red pegs, 5 square red pegs, 4 square yellow pegs, and 6 square blue pegs. One peg dropped out of the bag. What is the probability that it was red or round?

A $\frac{1}{10}$ **C** $\frac{7}{20}$

B $\frac{1}{4}$ **D** $\frac{1}{2}$

11. Which equation expresses the relationship between x and y shown in the table below?

x	y
0	0
1	5
3	15
8	40

F x = 5y   **H** x + y = 6
G y = 5x   **J** y − x = 4

Question 12 is an Extended Constructed Response Item.

12. Every Wednesday at the Pizza Express, the manager gives away free slices of pizza and soda. Every eighth customer gets a free slice of pizza and every twelfth customer gets a free soda. The Pizza Express served 87 customers last Wednesday.

- How many free sodas were given away last Wednesday?
- How many free slices of pizza were given away?
- Did any customer receive both a free slice of pizza and a free soda? If so, how many customers?
- If soda sells for 99¢ and a slice of pizza sells for $1.25, how much did the Pizza Express lose in income by giving away these items? Justify your answer.

Questions 13 through 15 are Student Produced Response Items.

13. If the dollar value of your investment is established by the formula I = p + prt, where p is the principal, r is the investment rate expressed as a decimal, and t is the amount of time in years, what is I when p = 600, r = 14%, and t = 3 years?

14. Jackson wants to earn money by washing cars. Shining Car Wash and Turtle Wax and Wash offer different salary plans. The graph below represents the salary schedule for each car wash.

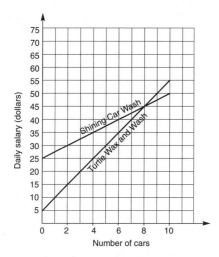

How many cars would Jackson have to wash in order to make the same salary in both car washes?

15. Delia surveyed 100 people about their choice of pizza toppings. Her results are shown in the table below.

Favorite Pizza Toppings

	Sausage	Pepperoni
Teens	36	14
Adults	28	22

If a teen is selected at random, what is the probability that the teen prefers pepperoni?

Question 16 is a Brief Constructed Response Item.

16. The appraised values of seven houses on the same block are given in the following chart.

Appraised Values: Block B	
#326	$350,000
#331	$378,500
#338	$343,800
#343	$355,900
#347	$363,500
#354	$358,000
#365	$786,500

• What is the difference between the mean and median values of the houses?
• Which measure, mean or median, is a better representation for the data and why?

17. In a football game, a field goal is kicked. The equation below describes the height of the ball, h, in feet, as a function of time, t, in seconds.

$$h(t) = 100t - 25t^2$$

What is the height of the ball after 2 seconds?

A 0 feet   **C** 75 feet

B 50 feet   **D** 100 feet

18. Mrs. Taylor bought a box of 48 packages of peanut butter crackers. Every day each of her five children ate one package of crackers for snack. Now there are 13 packs left. What equation can be used to find the number of days, n, that the children ate the crackers for snack?

F $48 = \dfrac{n}{5} - 13$ **H** $48 = \dfrac{n}{5} + 13$

G $48 = 5n - 13$ **J** $48 = 5n + 13$

19. Mr. Schwartz wants to order sweatshirts for the school store. Sweatshirts come in four colors: red, blue, green, and black. He randomly surveyed 50 students to determine which color sweatshirt they would buy. The table below shows the results.

Sweatshirt Color Votes

Color	Red	Blue	Green	Black
Number of Votes	15	14	6	15

Mr. Schwartz will order 350 sweatshirts. How many green sweatshirts should he order?

A 6   **B** 35   **C** 42   **D** 50

Session 2

20. What is the next term in this sequence?

$$2, 3\frac{1}{4}, 4\frac{1}{2}, 5\frac{3}{4}, \ldots$$

F $6\frac{1}{4}$ **G** $6\frac{1}{2}$ **H** $6\frac{3}{4}$ **J** 7

Question 21 is an Extended Constructed Response Item.

21. Miguel's scores in chemistry this quarter are 90, 30, 78, 75, 40, 54, 70.

- What is the median grade?
- What is the mean grade?
- Miguel decides to use the median grade to report to his parents, what advantage is there to his using the median rather than the mean?

22. Chris conducts a random survey of all the juniors to determine how many students like to go to baseball games. Which of the following methods would provide Chris with a simple random sample?

A Choose every 5th junior who goes to the baseball game.

B Survey the juniors in both the chess club and drama club.

C Choose every 3rd junior who enters the school until he has surveyed 25 students.

D Number every junior in the school and generate random numbers to select 50 students.

23. The graph below shows the population of a village since 2000. A curve of best fit is drawn.

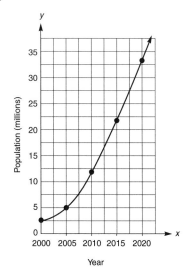

Year

According to the curve of best fit, what will the population be in the year 2012?

F 10 million

G 15 million

H 20 million

J 25 million

24. Which of the following numerical patterns is equivalent to this visual pattern?

A 0.33333 . . .

B 123123123 . . .

C 133133133 . . .

D 313131 . . .

25. Which of the graphs below shows the relationship between x and y shown in the table?

x	$^-1$	0	1	3	4
y	2	4	6	10	12

F

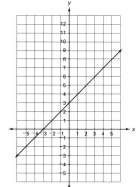

H

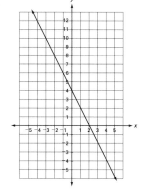

G

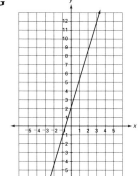

J

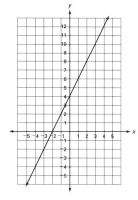

26. Michelle drops a ball from the roof of a 200-foot building. The graph below shows the relationship between the height of the ball and the distance, in feet, from the building.

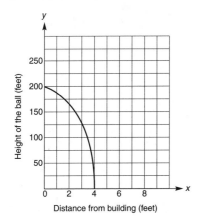

Distance from building (feet)

How far away from the building did the ball land?

A 2 feet   **C** 6 feet
B 4 feet   **D** 8 feet

27. Which equation describes the line shown below?

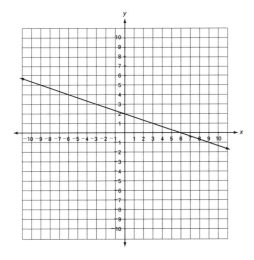

F $y = {}^-x + 3$ **H** $y = \frac{1}{3}x + 2$

G $y = \frac{-1}{3}x + 2$ **J** $y = x + 3$

28. A manager for a battery manufacturer randomly examined 10 groups of 12 batteries. The table below shows the number of defective batteries in each group she examined.

Box Number	1	2	3	4	5	6	7	8	9	10
Number of Defective Batteries	3	2	4	3	1	0	3	2	4	0

How many defective keys would be expected in a group of 480 batteries?

A 22   **B** 88   **C** 100   **D** 120

29. Jen and Ben dropped a ball from various heights and measured the height of the first bounce. They graphed their results below.

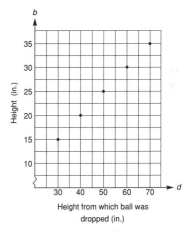

Height from which ball was dropped (in.)

Which equation best shows the relationship between the height from which the ball was dropped and the height of the ball's first bounce?

F $b = d - 20$ **H** $b = d + 20$

G $b = 2d$ **J** $b = \frac{1}{2}d$

Question 30 is an Extended Constructed Response Item.

30. Pauline purchased three bags of fudge and two cupcakes at a bakery for charged $5.90. Thomas purchased five bags of fudge and four cupcakes for $11.00.

- Write an equation that represents Pauline's total cost. Write an equation that represents Thomas' total cost.
- What is the cost of one bag of fudge? What is the cost of one cupcake? Use mathematics to justify your answers.
- Using your answers; find the cost of purchasing two bags of fudge and six cupcakes.

31. Find the missing term in the sequence shown below.

$$2, 5, 14, ?, 122, 365$$

A 27　　B 41　　C 75　　D 100

32. Look at the function that is graphed below.

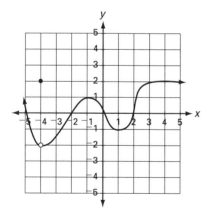

The function is not continuous at what x value?

F $^{-}4$　　G $^{-}2$　　H 2　　J 4

33. Statistics is the study of

A light bulbs　　C numerical data
B random samples　　D election polls

34. David and John left their house at the same time traveling in the same direction.

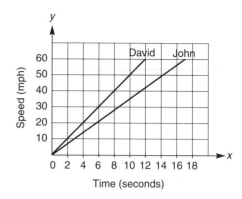

Who takes the least amount of time to go from 0 to 60 mph and about how much less time does it take?

F David by about 5 seconds
G John by about 5 seconds

H David by about $2\frac{1}{2}$ seconds

J John by about $2\frac{1}{2}$ seconds

Question 35 is a Brief Constructed Response Item.

35. The table gives the average weight for men of different heights. The data is for men with medium frames, ages 30 to 39 years old.

Height (in.)	Weight (lb)
64	145
66	153
68	161
70	170
72	179
74	188
76	199

- Write an equation for the line of best fit.
- According to your line of best fit, what is the average weight of a man 84 inches tall?

Questions 36 through 38 are Student Produced Response Items.

36. On a six-day vacation, Susan had a certain amount money to spend on souvenirs. On Sunday, the last night of her vacation, she had $2 left. As a matter of fact, each evening after the first she discovered that she had one-third the amount of money she had the previous evening. How much money did Susan start with?

37. If the pattern is continued, how many dots will be needed to represent the ninth term?

38. Suppose a dress code survey that included 200 men and 200 women had results as indicated in the table.

	For Stronger Dress Code	Against Stronger Dress Code	Total
Men	80	120	200
Women	110	90	200
Total	190	210	400

Find the probability that a person chosen at random, from among the 400 people, is a male against a stronger dress code.

39. The ages of five children in a family are 3, 3, 5, 8, and 18. Which statement is true for this group of data?

A mode > mean
B mean > median
C median = mode
D median > mean

40. Anthony and Laquisha have volunteered to serve on the Sophomore Prom Committee. The names of twenty volunteers, including Anthony and Laquisha, are put into a bowl. If two names are randomly drawn from the bowl without replacement, what is the probability that Anthony's will be drawn first and Laquisha's name will be drawn second?

F $\frac{1}{400}$　　　　H $\frac{2}{20}$

G $\frac{1}{380}$　　　　J $\frac{1}{200}$

41. On February 9, from 9 A.M. until 2 P.M., the temperature rose from ⁻14°F to 36°F. What was the total increase in temperature during this time period?

A 50°　　　　C 32°
B 36°　　　　D 22°

42. An equation of the line that has a slope of 3 and a y-intercept of ⁻2 is

F $x = 2y - 3$　　　　H $y = \frac{-2}{3}x$

G $y = 3x - 2$　　　　J $y = {}^{-}2x + 3$

Sample HSA Test 2

Session 1

1. The table below shows a relationship between *d* and *t*.

d	2	4	6	8	10	?
t	1	9	25	49	81	?

If the pattern continues, what are the next values for *d* and *t*?

A $d = 12, t = 100$
B $d = 12, t = 121$
C $d = 12, t = 144$
D $d = 12, t = 169$

2. Lisa saved $4x + 7$ dollars to spend on souvenirs. She spent $x - 3$ dollars on souvenirs for her brother. Which of these expressions represents the amount of money Lisa has left to spend on souvenirs?

F $(x - 3) + (4x + 7)$
G $(x - 3) - (4x + 7)$
H $(4x + 7) - (x - 3)$
J $(4x + 7)(x - 3)$

3. Which of the following tables corresponds to the line that is graphed below?

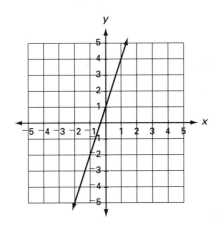

A

x	⁻2	0	1	2
y	7	4	1	⁻2

B

x	⁻2	0	1	2
y	⁻5	1	4	7

C

x	⁻4	⁻2	1	2
y	5	1	⁻5	⁻7

D

x	⁻4	⁻2	1	2
y	3	⁻1	⁻3	⁻9

4. Look at the graph of the function below.

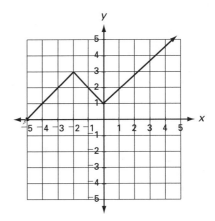

Between what interval is the function decreasing?

F $^-5 \leq x \leq {}^-2$
G $^-2 \leq x \leq 0$
H $2 \leq x \leq 3$
J $3 \leq x \leq 6$

5. At the end of the week, Samantha counts how many stuffed animals her toyshop has. The results for two weeks are shown in the matrices below. She did not receive any new stuffed animals during the two weeks.

Week 1	dog	bear	cat
S	38	45	55
M	20	28	30
L	15	20	30

Week 2	dog	bear	cat
S	20	28	43
M	8	20	22
L	9	15	24

How many more small bears than medium bears did she sell at the end of the second week?

A 28

B 20

C 17

D 9

Question 6 is a Brief Constructed Response Item

6. The science exam scores for 21 students in Mr. Nickelson's physics class were:

65 90 82 78 84 92 88 86 70 68 75
88 90 85 61 81 79 82 84 83 90

- What are the mean, median, and mode of the data?
- What is the best general indicator of this class's performance on the exam? Explain your answer.
- One student's score was miscalculated; the incorrect score is 61 and the correct score is 70. Does this correction have a greater influence on the mean or the median for the exam scores? Use mathematics to justify your answer.

7. Which pair of lines are perpendicular to each other and pass through the point $(0, {}^-5)$?

F $2y = x - 10$ and $2y = x + 10$

G $2y = x - 10$ and $^-2y = x + 10$

H $2y = x - 10$ and $y = 2x + 5$

J $2y = x - 10$ and $y = {}^-2x - 5$

8. Which of these graphs represents the solution set of the inequality $3x - 5y \leq 10$?

A

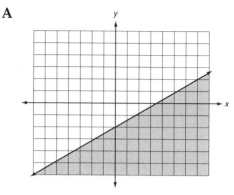

B

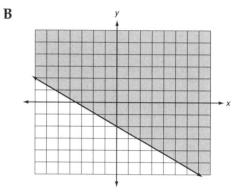

C

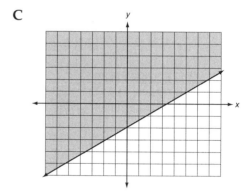

D

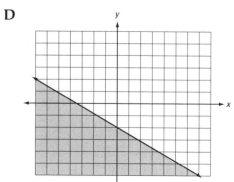

9. The chart below shows the total number of applications processed at the local Department of Motor Vehicles.

Applications Processed at the DMV

Time	Total Number of Applications Processed
9:00	15
9:30	30
10:00	45
10:30	60

If the pattern continues, what will the total number of applications processed by 12:30?

F 15
G 90
H 120
J 135

10. What is the minimum value of the function graphed below?

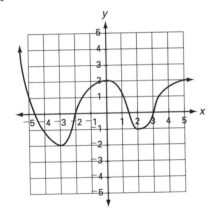

A ⁻5
B ⁻2
C 2
D 5

11. Dylan rolled a six-sided die 100 times and recorded his results in the table below.

Results of 100 Rolls

Side	Frequency
1	21
2	18
3	19
4	16
5	15
6	11

Based on the results in the table, how many times should Dylan expect the die to land on a 1 or a 6 if he rolls the die 500 times?

F 11
G 21
H 32
J 160

Question 12 is an Extended Constructed Response Item.

12. Suppose the pattern shown were continued.

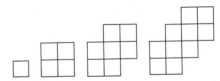

- Extend the pattern for two more terms.
- Write an expression that can be used to find the number of squares in the nth term.
- How many squares would be in the 100th diagram? Use mathematics to explain how you determined your answer.

Questions 13 through 15 are Student Produced Response Items.

13. A box contains colored jellybeans. There are 14 red, 6 yellow, and x green jellybeans in the bag. If the probability of drawing a yellow jellybean is $\frac{1}{4}$, how many green jellybeans are in the bag?

14. Amanda has 35 marbles in her collection. She collects 3 new marbles each week. In how many weeks will she have a total of 200 marbles in her collection?

15. Derek asked 250 students at his college their confidence of the school's basketball team winning the championship game. The results from his survey are shown below.

Survey Results

	Male	Female
Win	76	54
Lose	30	25
Not Sure	17	48

If a male student is selected at random, what is the probability that he is confident that the basketball team will win or lose?

Question 16 is a Brief Constructed Response Item.

16. Mr. McGraw records the number of miles traveled each time he fills up his gas tank. Let x represent the number of fill-ups. Let y represent the number of miles per gallon he gets. An equation for a line of best fit is shown below.

$$y = {}^-0.65x + 28$$

Answer the following:
- What is the slope of the line of best fit? In the context of this problem, what does the slope mean?
- What is the y-intercept of the line of best fit? In the context of this problem, what does the y-intercept mean?
- According to the line of best fit, how many miles per gallon did Mr. McGraw get on his 12th fill-up? Use mathematics to explain how you determined your answer.

17. A teacher tells a class that the median test grade was 83% and that 25% of the class had scores of 90% and higher. Robert had an 81% on his test. He scored

A in the lower 50% of the class
B in the upper 50% of the class
C in the first quartile
D in the third quartile

18. Which formula expresses the relationship between y and m shown in the table below?

y	2	3.5	5	7
m	24	42	60	84

F $y = 12m$ H $m = 12y$

G $m = y + 20$ J $y = \frac{1}{2}m$

19. First-class postage for items that weigh up to one ounce is $0.39. Each additional ounce, or fraction of an ounce, cost $0.24. The graph represents the cost of mailing a first-class item depending on the weight of that item in ounces.

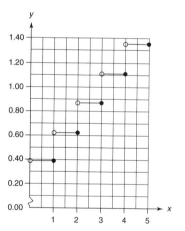

What is the cost to mail a letter that weighed 3.2 ounces?

A $0.39   C $0.87

B $0.63   D $1.11

Session 2

20. A box contains 50 marbles: 25 are red, 15 are white, and 10 are blue. Wilson took a marble without looking. What is the probability that the marble is <u>not</u> blue?

F .30   **G** .40   **H** .50   **J** .80

Question 21 is an Extended Constructed Response Item.

21. Marta has $24 to spend on souvenirs. Mugs cost $4 each, including tax, and posters cost $2 each, including tax.

Answer the following:
- Let x represent the number of posters and y represent the number of mugs. Write an inequality that represents the situation above.
- What is the <u>maximum</u> number of posters Marta can buy if she buys 3 mugs? Use mathematics to explain how you determined your answer.
- List all the number combinations of posters and mugs Marta can buy to spend <u>exactly</u> $24. Use mathematics to justify your answer.

22. The graph below shows the path a football travels, horizontally, after it is kicked.

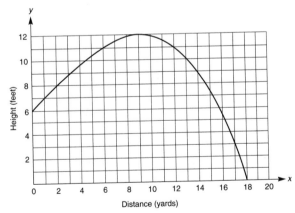

How far does the football travel before it hits the ground?

A 4 yards
B 18 yards
C 20 yards
D 25 yards

23. The temperature, T, in degrees Celsius, at a depth, d, in kilometers, inside Earth is given by the equation

$$T = 10d + 20$$

Which graph best represents this relationship?

F
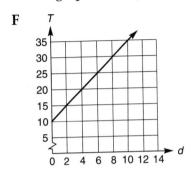

G
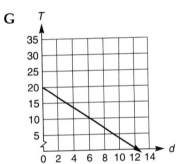

H
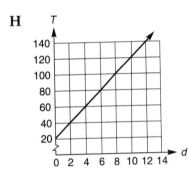

J
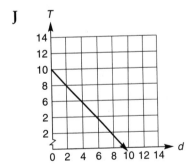

24. Which expression tells how much money a shopper has left if x represents the amount the shopper started with and s represents the amount spent before a 25% discount?

A $C = x - s$

B $C = x - 0.25s$

C $C = x + 0.25s$

D $C = x - 0.75s$

25. The distance Mrs. Jacob traveled one Saturday afternoon while running errands is shown in the graph below.

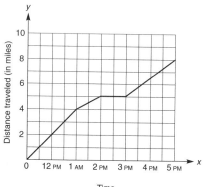

Time

What was most likely happening between 2:00 and 3:00 P.M.?

F Mrs. Jacob was in heavy traffic.

G Mrs. Jacob had stopped for lunch.

H Mrs. Jacob was looking for a parking place downtown.

J Mrs. Jacob was traveling on a highway.

26. The video game JP wants to buy costs at least $50 and not more than $70. He earns $7 as a part-time receptionist in an office. Which of the following inequalities shows the number of hours, n, he will have to work to pay for the game?

A $7n \geq 20$

B $\dfrac{n}{7} \geq 20$

C $50 \leq 7n \leq 70$

D $50 \leq \dfrac{n}{7} \leq 20$

27. A game designer is creating a baseball simulation. The mechanism for randomizing is a die with 20 sides: two zeros, two 1s, two 2s ... two 9s. In baseball, a ".300 hitter" averages 3 hits for every 10 official at-bats. Which would correctly simulate a .300 hitter?

F 0, 1, or 2 represent a hit and 3, 4, 5, 6, 7, 8, or 9 represent an out

G 1 or 2 represent a hit and 3 through 9 or 0 represent an out

H 0, 1, 2, or 3 represent a hit and 4 through 9 represent an out

J 3, 6, or 9 represent a hit and 0, 2, 4, or 8 represent an out

28. The matrix below shows the two video rental plans Kip's Video Store offers.

$$\begin{array}{c@{\quad}cc} & \text{Plan A} & \text{Plan B} \\ \text{Annual Fee} & \$20.00 & \$0.00 \\ \text{Daily Rental} & \$1.99 & \$2.59 \end{array}$$

Chrystie's Video Store also has video rental plans but their prices are 3% more than the prices at Kip's. Which of the follow matrices represents the rental plans at Chrystie's?

A
$$\begin{array}{c@{\quad}cc} & \text{Plan A} & \text{Plan B} \\ \text{Annual Fee} & \$0.60 & \$0.00 \\ \text{Daily Rental} & \$0.06 & \$0.08 \end{array}$$

B
$$\begin{array}{c@{\quad}cc} & \text{Plan A} & \text{Plan B} \\ \text{Annual Fee} & \$0.60 & \$0.03 \\ \text{Daily Rental} & \$0.06 & \$0.08 \end{array}$$

C
$$\begin{array}{c@{\quad}cc} & \text{Plan A} & \text{Plan B} \\ \text{Annual Fee} & \$20.60 & \$0.00 \\ \text{Daily Rental} & \$2.05 & \$2.67 \end{array}$$

D
$$\begin{array}{c@{\quad}cc} & \text{Plan A} & \text{Plan B} \\ \text{Annual Fee} & \$20.60 & \$0.03 \\ \text{Daily Rental} & \$2.05 & \$2.67 \end{array}$$

29. The graph shows the relationship between distance and time.

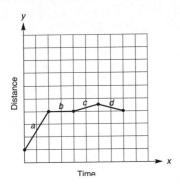

Which statement is false?

F Segment *a* shows a sharp increase in distance.

G Segment *b* shows distance remaining constant.

H Segment *c* shows a gradual increase in distance.

J Segment *d* shows a sharp decrease in distance.

Question 30 is an Extended Constructed Response Item.

30. Kimberly asked 150 randomly selected customers at a music store how much they spent on CDs from the store. The survey results are shown in the table below.

Amount Spent	Number of Customers
$0	25
$0.01–$5.99	17
$6.00–$9.99	32
$10.00–$19.99	15
$20.00–$49.99	45
$50.00–$99.99	10
$100 and over	6

Answer the following:

• Five hundred customers shopped at the music store in one month. Based on the survey results, how many customers spent between $20.00 and $49.99 at the store? Use mathematics to justify your answer.

• Using the results from the survey, Kimberly concluded that 4 more people will spend between $50.00 and $99.99 at the music store than those who will spend $100 and over. Is Kimberly's conclusion correct? Justify your answer.

• Calvin conducted the same survey at the music store when the store had its annual sale. Will Calvin's survey or Kimberly's survey give more reliable results?

31. The mean score on Thursday's chemistry test was 85.5%. Twenty-six students took the test on Thursday. Two students who took a makeup test on Friday scored 73% and 56%. As a result, the mean score for all 28 students

A stayed the same

B fell 1.5%

C rose slightly

D fell 14%

32. On a production line, 26 leaky batteries were found amount 2,000 randomly selected batteries. How many leaky batteries will there be if 10,000 batteries are selected?

F 26

G 130

H 2,000

J 10,000

33. How much Jeremy will pay each month, C, depends on the number, n, of long distance calls he makes. This relationship is represented by the equation.

$$C = 0.05n + 29.95$$

What is the significance of the slope of this equation?

A Jeremy will be charged $0.05 less a minute for long distance calls.

B Jeremy will be charged an additional $0.05 a minute for long distance calls.

C Jeremy will have to pay $29.95 each month before making any long distance calls.

D Jeremy will only have to pay $29.95 a month for his long distance calls.

34. The box-and-whisker plots below show the data on injury ratings for cars.

Injury Ratings for Two-Door Autos

Large

Midsize

Small

60 70 80 90 100 110 120 130 140 150 160

Which conclusion seems to be supported by these box-and-whisker plots?

F The chance of injury tends to decrease as the size of the car increases.

G The chance of injury tends to increase with the size of the car.

H The outlier for small cars has a much higher injury rating than other small cars have.

J Midsize cars show the most variability in injury ratings.

Question 35 is a Brief Constructed Response Item.

35. The weekly salaries of six employees in a small firm are $340, $345, $345, $350, $350, and $520.

• Find the mean, median, and mode for all six of these salaries.

• If negotiations for new salaries are in session and you represent management, which measure of central tendency will you use as the average salary? Use mathematics to explain your answer.

Questions 36 through 38 are Student Produced Response Items.

36. Look at the sequence below.

1, 3, 27, 256, . . .

What is the next term in this sequence?

37. If Ben is presently 22 years old and his sister Christina is 12 years old, in how many years will Christina be $\frac{2}{3}$ as old as Ben?

38. An arrow is shot into the air at an angle. Its height, in feet, depends on the time, t, in seconds it is in flight. The formula below is used to calculate the height of the arrow.

$$h = 40 + 120t - 4t^2$$

What is the height of the arrow after it has been in flight for 5 seconds?

39. Which number is in the solution set of the inequality $5x + 3 > 38$?

A 5   **B** 6   **C** 7   **D** 8

40. John left his home and walked 3 blocks to his school, as shown in the accompanying graph.

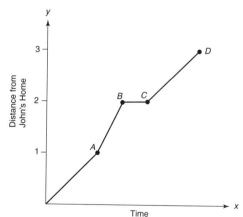

What is one possible interpretation of the section of the graph from point B to point C?

F John arrived at school and stayed throughout the day.

G John waited before crossing a busy street.

H John returned home to get his algebra homework.

J John reached the top of a hill and began walking on level ground.

41. Tara buys two items that cost d dollars each. She gives the cashier $20. Which expression represents the change she should receive?

A $20 - 2d$

B $20 - d$

C $20 + 2d$

D $2d - 20$

42. At the beginning of her mathematics class, Mrs. Reno gives a Do Now problem. She says, "I am thinking of a number such that 6 less than the product of 7 and this number is 85." Which number is she thinking of?

F 10

G 13

H 91

J 84

Session 1

1. The graph below shows the monthly sales for Sparkle Jewelry for 2005.

Sparkle Jewelry Monthly Sales

What was the change in sales from October to November?

A increased about $13,000
B increased about $20,000
C decreased about $8,000
D stayed about the same

2. Jonathan and Anthony both have a quarter pound of candy. Jonathan has 5 jelly beans and 2 gumballs, and Anthony has 2 jelly beans and 3 gumballs. Which of the following shows the relationship between the weights of one gumball and one jelly bean?

F 1 jelly bean weighs the same as 1 gumball
G 1 gumball weighs the same as 3 jelly beans
H 2 gumballs weigh the same as 4 jelly beans
J 5 jelly beans weigh the same as 3 gumballs

3. The following data resulted from a chemistry experiment: 0.03 gram, 1.4 grams, 3.8 grams, 2.8 grams, 3.8 grams. What would the sixth data value be if the mean of this experiment was 2.1 grams?

A 1.57 g   **C** 0.77 g
B 0.80 g   **D** 0.71 g

4. The matrix below represents the regular price of lawn furniture.

$$\begin{array}{c c c c}
 & \text{Chair} & \text{Table} & \text{Ottoman} \\
\text{Unpainted} & \left[\begin{array}{ccc} \$65.00 & \$95.00 & \$25.00 \\ \$79.00 & \$120.00 & \$32.00 \end{array}\right. \\
\text{Painted} & & &
\end{array}$$

At the end-of-the-season sale, unpainted lawn furniture is reduced 50% and painted lawn furniture is reduced 40% off of the regular price. Which matrix represents the sale price for each type of furniture?

F $\left[\begin{array}{ccc} \$39.00 & \$57.00 & \$15.00 \\ \$47.40 & \$72.00 & \$19.20 \end{array}\right]$

G $\left[\begin{array}{ccc} \$32.50 & \$47.50 & \$12.50 \\ \$47.40 & \$72.00 & \$19.20 \end{array}\right]$

H $\left[\begin{array}{ccc} \$32.50 & \$47.50 & \$12.50 \\ \$39.50 & \$60.00 & \$16.00 \end{array}\right]$

J $\left[\begin{array}{ccc} \$26.00 & \$38.00 & \$10.00 \\ \$39.50 & \$60.00 & \$16.00 \end{array}\right]$

5. The Hill Lightbulb Company tests 5% of their daily production of lightbulbs. If 500 bulbs were tested on Thursday, what was the total number of bulbs produced that day?

A 25   **C** 10,000
B 1,000   **D** 100,000

Question 6 is a Brief Constructed Response Item.

6. A store manager made a frequency table of the sizes of men's shirts sold in one week.

Shirts Sold	
Size	Frequency
14	2
$14\frac{1}{2}$	5
15	10
$15\frac{1}{2}$	19
16	7
$16\frac{1}{2}$	4
17	1

Answer the following:

- Find the mean, median, and mode of the data.
- Which measure of central tendency is most useful for the manager when ordering new shirts? Why? Use mathematics to justify your answer.

7. A farmer has a rectangular field that measures 100 feet by 150 feet. He plans to increase the area of the field by 20%. He will do this by increasing the length and width by the same amount, x. Which equation represents the area of the new field?

  F $(100 + 2x)(150 + x) = 18,000$
  G $2(100 + x) + 2(150 + x) = 15,000$
  H $(100 + x)(150 + x) = 18,000$
  J $(100 + x)(150 + x) = 15,000$

8. A basketball player has a career average of 70 percent at the free-throw line. Which of the following would simulate the player's making a free throw?

  A Roll a 10-sided die, numbered 0–9. Let an even number represent a free throw made.
  B Flip a coin 10 times. Let tails represent free throws made.

  C Spin a spinner with equal sections numbered 1 through 10. Let an odd number represent free throws made.
  D Draw from cards numbered 1 through 10. Let the numbers 4 through 10 represent free throws made.

9. Amanda has a 10-question quiz on Thursday. Her father agrees to give her on Sunday her regular $5 allowance plus $0.75 for each question she answered correctly on Thursday's quiz. However, he will not give Amanda anymore than twice her allowance. Which inequality below best represents the situation described above?

  F $0.75n \leq 10$
  G $5 - 0.75n \leq 10$
  H $0.75n + 5 \leq 10$
  J $(0.75 + 5)n \leq 10$

10. Look at the pattern below.
  $3, 9, 27, \ldots$
  If this pattern is continued, what is the tenth term?

  A 2,187
  B 6,561
  C 19,683
  D 59,049

11. Which inequality is graphed below?

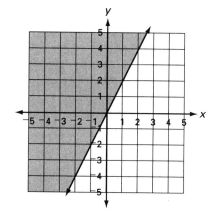

  F $y \geq x + 2$
  G $y \leq 2x$
  H $y \geq 2 - x$
  J $y \geq 2x$

Question 12 is an Extended Constructed Response Item.

12. The games at Happy Pappy's World of Fun Restaurant require exact dollar change or tokens to play. The staffers conducted a random survey of 200 children to determine which way they paid to play the games. The results from the survey are shown in the table below.

Number of Children Who Used Dollars	Number of Children Who Use Tokens
112	88

- Over the weekend 700 children went to Happy Pappy's World of Fun. Based on the results from the survey, how many of the children would be expected to use tokens to pay for the games they played? Use mathematics to justify your answer.
- On Saturday, Matt reported that 143 children used tokens to pay for the games they played. Based on the results from the survey, how many children went to Happy Pappy's World of Fun. Use mathematics to justify your answer.
- If there was a party of 150 children at Lily Hop Restaurant, should staffers use the above survey results to predict the number of children who used dollars to play games at the restaurant? Justify your answer.

Questions 13 through 15 are Student Produced Response Items.

13. The matrices below show how many of each type of food was sold at a college and high school basketball game and at a football game.

Basketball Game

	H.S.	College
Hot Dogs	144	305
Hamburgers	215	114
Sodas	505	423
Chips	413	405

Football Game

	H.S.	College
Hot Dogs	258	564
Hamburgers	195	125
Sodas	600	753
Chips	332	658

How many high school and college students prefer hamburgers at the basketball and football games?

14. From a club of 21 students; 12 girls and 9 boys, two students will be randomly selected to serve as president and vice president. What is the probability that two girls will be selected?

15. Currently, Tyrone has $60 and his sister has $130. Both get an allowance of $5 each week. Tyrone decides to save is entire allowance, but his sister spends all of hers each week plus an additional $10 each week. After how many weeks will they have the same amount of money?

Question 16 is a Brief Constructed Response Item.

16. Gloria decided to keep a record of how much gas she uses. Each time she puts gas in the car, she records the number of gallons of gas purchased and the number of miles driven since the last fill-up. Below is her record for the first month.

Gallons of Gas	Miles Driven
9	290
10	324
12	415
11	350
7	240
6	200

Answer the following:

- Find the equation for a line of best fit for this data.
- What is the slope of the equation you found? What does the slope represent in the context of this problem?
- The next time Gloria fills up the car, she purchased 4 gallons of gas. According to your equation for the line of best fit, what is the number of miles she drove since her previous fill-up? Use mathematics to justify your answer.

17. What is the number of zeros of the function shown below?

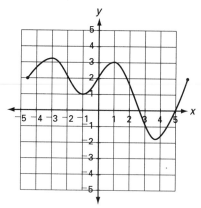

A 3   **B** 2   **C** 1   **D** 0

18. A waitress surveyed 60 people about the type of juice they drink in the morning. The results are shown in the table below.

Juice	Number
apple	13
orange	21
grapefruit	11
cranberry	6
tomato	5
mango	4

If 150 people ate at the diner one morning, how many people would be expected to order mango juice?

F 5   **G** 10   **H** 15   **J** 20

19. The accompanying graph shows the amount of water left in Rover's water dish over a period of time.

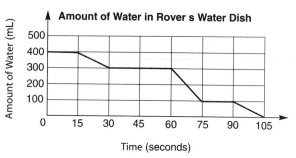

How long did Rover wait from the end of his first drink to the start of his second drink of water?

A 10 seconds   **C** 60 seconds
B 30 seconds   **D** 5 seconds

Session 2

20. 1,376 students attending Northeastern High School all voted for president of the Student Body. With approximately one-fifth of the votes counted, Jeremy, the leading candidate, had 185 votes. Assuming Jeremy obtained the same proportion of the total number of votes, the number of votes he received would be between

    F 900 and 950   **H** 450 and 500
    G 600 and 700   **J** 250 and 300

Question 21 is an Extended Constructed Response Item.

21. A candy store sells 32-ounce bags of a mixture of chocolate and raisins. The price of the 32-ounce bag depends upon the amount of chocolate. If c ounces of chocolate are in the bags, the price, p, can be expressed as $p = 0.2c + 0.1(32 - c)$.

    • Find the price of a bag containing 24 ounces of chocolate.
    • Find the price of a bag containing 24 ounces of raisins.
    • Katie spent $4.20 on her purchase. Describe the mixture she bought.

22. The Straight as an Arrow Company paints lines on the streets of different towns. The company charges $100 plus $0.25 per foot. Which of the following is a reasonable graph for length vs. total charge?

A

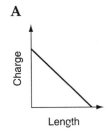

C

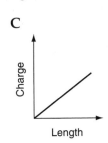

B

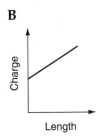

D

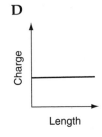

23. The accompanying graph shows the closing price per share of a certain stock over a period of seven days.

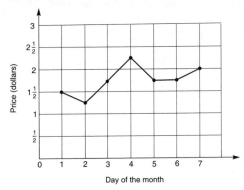

Between what two days did the price decrease most sharply?

F Between days 1 and 2
G Between days 2 and 3
H Between days 4 and 5
J Between days 5 and 6

24. The whole numbers from 1 to 40 are each written on a small slip of paper and placed in a box. One slip of paper is selected at random from the box. What is the probability that the number selected is prime if you are given that it is a factor of 36?

A 0   **C** $\dfrac{1}{18}$

B $\dfrac{1}{20}$ **D** $\dfrac{2}{9}$

25. A printing company makes bumper stickers that cost $0.75 per copy plus a $5.00 set-up fee. If you spend $80 to purchase a supply of bumper stickers, how many do you get?

    F 50   **H** 100
    G 75   **J** 150

26. In 2004, Louis bought a car for $x^3 - 6x$ dollars. One year later the value of the car was $x^2 + 8$ dollars. Which expression represents the amount that the car value decreased?

A $(x^2 + 8) \times (x^3 - 6x)$
B $(x^3 - 6x) \div (x^2 + 8)$
C $(x^2 + 8) - (x^3 - 6x)$
D $(x^3 - 6x) - (x^2 + 8)$

27. In the past three censuses, the populations of Towns A and B grew. Town A's population counts were 47,157, 63,285, and 73,913. Town B's population counts were 37,780, 55,783, and 68,040. If there is a fourth census and Town B's population is 80,145, what would Town A's population have to be in order to have a higher mean for all four censuses?

F Less than 57,393
G Greater than 57,393
H Equal to 57,393
J Not equal to 57,393

28. Look at the graph of a function below.

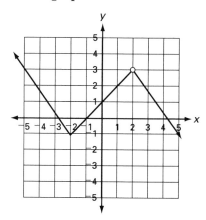

The function is not continuous at x equals

A 2   C 5
B 3   D 8

29. The area of a rectangular field is 540 square yards and its width is 9 yards. What is the length of the field?

F 6 yards
G 9 yards
H 60 yards
J 90 yards

Question 30 is an Extended Constructed Response Item.

30. The length of a spring is related to the weight that hangs from it. The table below shows the relationship between the length, l, in centimeters and the weight, w, in kilograms, of a spring.

w	l
2	14
3	16
5	20
6	22
8	26
11	32

- According to the pattern shown in the table, what would the length of the spring if the weight is 15 kilograms?
- Write an algebraic expression that would represent the relationship between the length of the spring and the weight.
- If the weight is 25 kilograms, what would the length of the spring be? Use mathematics to justify your answer.

31. Which line has a slope of $-\dfrac{2}{3}$ and a y-intercept of 2?

A $2y = {}^-3x + 4$
B $3x + 2y = 6$
C $2x + 3y = 6$
D $3y = 2x - 6$

32. Which of the following terms could not be a term of the sequence $\dfrac{1}{4}, \dfrac{1}{2}, 1, 2, \ldots$?

F 16   H 84
G 32   J 128

33. The table below shows the relationship between c and d.

c	d
0	20.00
1	21.50
2	23.00
3	24.50

  A $d = 1.50c$
  B $d = 1.50c + 20.00$
  C $d = 20.00c + 1.50$
  D $d = 21.50c$

34. On Veterans Day, 475 people caught the matinee show. Admission to the show was $7.00 for adults and $4.50 for children. The total receipts were $2,667.50. Which system of equations describes the number of adult tickets, a and the number of child tickets, c, purchased?

  F $a + c = 475$
  $a = \$2,667.50 - 2.50c$
  G $ac = 475$
  $\$7.00 + \$4.50c = \$2,667.50$
  H $a + c = 475$
  $\$7.00a + \$4.50c = \$2,667.50$
  J $\$7.00a + \$4.50c = 475$
  $a + c = \$2,667.50$

Questions 35 is a Brief Constructed Response Item.

35. A candy store sells 8-pound bags of mixed hazelnuts and cashews. If c pounds of cashews are in a bag, the price p of the bag can be found using the formula $p = 2.59c + 1.72(8 - c)$. If one bag is priced at $18.11, how many pounds of cashews does it contain?

Questions 36 through 38 are Student Produced Response Items.

36. Justin spent an evening playing video games and drinking sodas. Each video game cost 50 cents to play, and sodas cost 75 cents each. Justin had $12 to spend only on video games and sodas. If he had only 3 sodas and played as many video games as he could, what was the maximum number of video games he played?

37. The number of people on the school board is represented by x. Two subcommittees with an equal number of members are formed, one with $\frac{2}{3}x - 5$ members and the other with $\frac{x}{4}$ members. How many people are on the school board?

38. Selena and Tracey play on a softball team. Selena has 8 hits out of 20 times at bat, and Tracey has 6 hits out of 16 times at bat. Based on their past performances, what is the probability that both girls will get a hit next time at bat?

39. The line $3x - 2y = 12$ has

  A a slope of $\frac{3}{2}$ and a y-intercept of $^-6$
  B a slope of $-\frac{3}{2}$ and a y-intercept of 6
  C a slope of 3 and a y-intercept of $^-2$.
  D a slope of $^-3$ and a y-intercept of $^-6$

40. Rosario and Enrique are in the same algebra class. On the first five tests, Rosario received scores of 78, 77, 64, 86, and 70. Enrique received scores of 90, 61, 79, 73, and 87. How much higher was Enrique's average than Rosarios' average?

  F 15 points
  G 4 points
  H 3 points
  J 2 points

41. Junior had a 12-game bowling average of 140. He scored 179 in his next game. What was his new average?

  A 141.6   **C** 154.9
  B 143.0   **D** 159.5

42. On a poster; a picture that is actually 20 millimeters wide is shown 1 foot wide. If the picture is actually 30 millimeters long, how long is it on the poster?

  F $\frac{2}{3}$ ft   **H** $1\frac{1}{3}$ ft
  G $\frac{3}{4}$ ft   **J** $1\frac{1}{2}$ ft

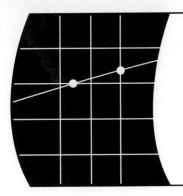

Index